Enjoy the Ride!

William Shawn Tillman

Enjoy the Ride!

William Shawn Tillman

Foreword by Karleigh Frisbie Brogan

SOME
PEOPLE
PRESS

Published by Some People Press
PO Box 12453, Portland, Oregon 97212

ISBN: 979-8-9941977-1-4

Cover and book design by Stuart Smith based on the series design
    by Laura Glazer
Editing by Harrell Fletcher
Copy editing by Kristi Garced
Proofreading by Gretchen Dykstra
Original text typed by Jordan Baseman, Madison East, Erika Jensen,
Prudence Roberts, Stephanie Silenti, Kierrin Viall

The image on pages x–xi is a facsimile of a page from one of the
author's notebooks in which he wrote his life story.

www.somepeoplepress.com
@somepeoplepress

Contents

A Note from the Publishers

Since the summer of 2022, we have run a weekly autobiographical writing and publishing workshop at the Columbia River Correctional Institution, a minimum-security prison for men in Northeast Portland, Oregon. It operates similarly to writing workshops in other contexts, where participants write during the week, read their work during class, and receive feedback. We bring in writing materials, books for inspiration, and visitors who have experience as writers, editors, and publishers. One of us worked for many years with the same prison to create an artist residency for inmates, and a comedy school for those who aspired to do stand-up.

More than sixty men have participated in the writing workshop so far. Some have been released and are completing their books on the outside, while others have drifted out of the program or been transferred to other prisons. Everyone who has attempted to write their life story has been unique and represented underrecognized perspectives on society, culture, ethics, and compassion.

Enjoy the Ride! is the fifth book in our Same Time series (we have published other books not related to the prison as part of our Other Places series). It was written by William Shawn Tillman, who joined the workshop about six months after it started and spent close to a year writing his autobiography.

Tillman's life has been filled with adventures and hard times, but his writing is surprisingly even handed and straightforward. He has led a life of deprivations, addictions, and struggles, but has also had experiences of beauty, grace, and incredible resilience.

—Harrell Fletcher and Laura Glazer

Foreword by Karleigh Frisbie Brogan

"In the day we sweat it out on the streets of a runaway
American dream. At night we ride through mansions
of glory in suicide machines."

— Bruce Springsteen, "Born to Run"

William Shawn Tillman started running when he was a young boy. The corner store with its candy bars and blue Blow Pops became a refuge from his unsafe home, his abusive and neglectful parents. His seventeenth year marked the beginning of his flight—a decades-long string of train-hopping, hitchhiking, and joyriding. Stolen cars became borrowed dreams, time machines. He'd run them up and down the West Coast, not fleeing trouble but chasing purpose. Every unlocked vehicle was a gift from God, carrying the potential of a new beginning or a shift in perspective, a return to an old and scant feeling of connection with humanity and nature—something, finally, to look forward to.

Tillman's is the literalization of every American's story. It's about the endless pursuit and the repetitive days, strong morals and even stronger justifications. It's about foolhardy hope on an empty tank.

Like Tillman, I yo-yoed between Oregon and California for over a decade before I finally realized that home would never be what it used to be, or, at least, what I'd recalled it to be with flawed nostalgia. In my many homecomings, it wasn't so much specific people or places I was hoping to reunite with, but feelings. Perhaps, too, I thought by returning, I could redo my troubled past, my bad decisions. I got involved with Some People Press after my memoir came out. It's a book that starts and ends at a gas station in Northern California, passersby filling up on their way to more exciting places than my suburban hometown, I imagined. I liked the fantasy of other people's fantasies. I watched as they merged back onto the

101, headed to headlands, maybe, to big cities or even bigger forests. Like Tillman, I was a thief and an addict. Like Tillman, I wanted to be accepted and respected and loved. I wanted to be understood. Though I've never met him, I understand his desires and his setbacks. I understand him.

I didn't know the writing workshop at Columbia River Correctional Institution was the missing piece in my life until I visited, until I listened to the words of men who had played the same game that society sanctions, but with different pieces. Many of these men got a raw deal from the jump because of the color of their skin or the parents they were born to or the poverty they endured. I didn't even know the prison existed, seven miles from my house off an outskirts road that threads between a border river and the airport runway. It was there all along, its residents, some of them, with ballpoint pens and dog-eared books, with yesterdays worth revisiting, worth unraveling—with something to look forward to.

Karleigh Frisbie Brogan is the author of Holding: A Memoir About Mothers, Drugs, and Other Comforts. *She was a 2024 Oregon Literary Fellow and the recipient of the 2023 George Pascoe Miller Scholarship and a 2022 Rona Jaffe Scholarship for the Bread Loaf Writers' Conference. She is from Santa Rosa, California, and currently resides in Portland, Oregon.*

Something you nee
garbage is anothe
was hoping to ge
kept hinting on th
was more interestin
had every excuse
coming up I gave
trying to get laid
preparing my self fo
I stoped at hon
Cen of my favirat
was a Dust off
unstopable, invisible,
Control all things o
the can like a wsh
in home Depo par
Civic, I take a blas
wam, wolves hit then

man, one mans
ans treasure, I
d that night I
subject, But she
n getting high and
to, As the sun was
on the idea of
turned to metally
re long Day, So
Jeps to Buy a
Drug of choice wich
a Bust off I was
seemed I could
el me, After hitting
r, So Im sitting
y lot in my honde
t the Cas and the
the rainbow colors

Chapter 1

My life so far has by no means been anything to brag about. In fact, the thirty-six years I've lived so far have been mostly hell. Quite frankly, the only excitement I've really had has been with the women I've slept with, the drugs I've taken, and yes, the cars I've stolen. Those times were my freest—nothing holding me back, no one in control of my life but me.

It's very hard to say I'll never engage in those activities again. I'm only human, and those were the times that really let me really know that I am.

But, at this certain point in my life, I realize the decisions I've made in the past are the reasons for me being in prison right now, which is where I'm writing this book.

I call those past decisions and experiences my trials and tribulations. I know one thing for sure though: I was never going to be killed or outsmarted by the devil's evil deeds or tricks. I stayed three steps ahead of him and that helped me avoid any real dangers or disasters.

The devil couldn't play me like a fool. I called his bluff every time, which only made him madder. I won the battles by simply staying alive and maintaining my ability to think for myself. It was always just Satan trying to pull me away from the spiritual journey I was on. What the devil didn't know was that we were already one, me and God.

Chapter 2

As a child living in Moreno Valley, California, I was already taking care of my younger sister and brother. We were eight, six, and four—each of us two years apart. We ran around in the streets in nothing but long T-shirts—no pants, socks, or shoes. We were dirty from head to toe, and had ice cream stains around our mouths. Grime ran all the way down the fronts of our shirts and we always had dirty feet. We'd toss any glass bottles we found on the road over fences into someone else's property, just so we could hear the shatter sound on the other side, never knowing who or what might have been over there.

I remember we were always trying to get dollar food stamps, the old brown ones that came in a book once a month. When we'd get a few food stamp dollars together, we'd run away from home. I guess it wasn't actually "running away from home" because our mom knew we were just going down to the store for candy.

My favorite was the blueberry suckers with gum on the inside. I'd get four of them for a dollar. That was winning back then, or so I thought. The store was just two or three blocks away. My mom didn't mind—hell, she was probably happy we were out of her hair and not interrupting the partying she was doing with her boyfriends over at the house. Her favorite line to yell at us was, "If you're coming in, you're staying in," and since us kids never wanted to be inside, we were outside most of the time.

We were only in the house when we got in trouble. Those memories really suck to think back on, so I won't, not now anyway, but like a horror film they play back in my mind sometimes.

I do think it's important to explain a little bit about how abnormal my childhood was though. Maybe it'll make the rest of the story make more sense. I'm just starting to understand how growing up that way impacted the rest of my life.

With little supervision, my siblings and I were always doing something wrong, which was not completely our fault, because our parents didn't raise us right. We were verbally abused, sexually abused, and suffered from extreme abandonment and neglect.

As a kid I was confused, lost, and always scared—not only for my life, but for the lives of my younger sister and brother too. There were cul-de-sacs at both ends of the street we lived on, another street ran into it like a T. Every day in that neighborhood there were drive-by shootings, people fighting, and people dying. The Blacks were at one end and the Mexicans at the other and we were caught right in the middle, literally. The alley behind our house became our playground. It was safer back there.

One time I got chased out of the real playground at the daycare center down the street. It was fenced up and closed after hours but other kids still played there. I got hit by a huge rock when I tried to jump over the fence to get in one time. I didn't understand why I couldn't play with the other kids, and why they wanted to hurt me. I know now it was because of the race war that was taking place.

I ended up with a huge cut across my head. The next thing I knew, I was in an ambulance going to the hospital with a concussion and needing stitches.

From then on I pretty much played alone or just with my sister and brother. It was experiences like that, the violence I encountered at such a young age, that set the rest of my life in motion. It impacted me in ways I couldn't understand at that age, and I didn't have parents who could help me make sense of it. All I wanted to do was have fun like the other kids.

My parents were always getting high on heroin, crack, or meth, and getting drunk and having sex (with each other or other people).

Emotionally I've struggled through life not really knowing who I am or who to trust. It takes me a long time to warm up to people I don't know. I realize I've missed a lot of opportunities that could have possibly set my life in different directions. I can only look at those obstacles now as lessons though—I got to learn things the hard way.

It's a perfect example of cause and effect. My parents had messed up lives so that's what they offered up to us, but I'm trying to not repeat the process I went through with my own child. My son, who is ten now, needs me to be a real father and teach him everything about life, all the things I was never taught. I can't wait to get out of prison so I can go see him. I love my son, and I want to give him all my attention.

Chapter 3

A turning point happened in my life one day. It was the last time anyone would see us kids running and playing in the streets of Moreno Valley. My mom's dad, Wayne, and his wife Julie heard what was going on—about how us three kids were not being properly taken care of. We were basically picked up by two strangers we'd never met in our entire lives, but they turned out to be my grandpa and grandma.

They put us in their car and drove us all the way north, over 500 miles, to Humboldt County, and a tiny town called Bridgeville, with a population of just a few hundred people spread throughout the woods. The closest shopping center was about a thirty-minute drive away.

My brother, sister, and I had never been out of the city before and hadn't even really ridden in cars much. We didn't know what was happening. We had to trust those people who picked us up out of our crazy lives and hope they'd give us a new life, and that they wouldn't try to harm us in some way.

You can imagine that at the age of eight, with my sister six, and my brother four—we were all really scared by what was happening. Our parents weren't good parents, but they were all we knew. My grandparents had a huge job on their hands. I don't think they knew what they were getting themselves into when they took custody of us.

We were bad little kids. We would be cursing every time things didn't go our way. We had no manners and were used to running wild. But it didn't matter. We were family. Our grandparents loved kids, especially their own grandkids. My grandpa was disabled though, and in a wheelchair. That put a lot more stress on my grandmother to try to raise us kids mostly on her own. My grandma's mom, who also lived with us, was in a wheelchair too, so there was a lot of work to be done.

As we grew up, we became care providers and helped my grandpa and grandma's mom with their daily needs, including feeding them, scratching their itchy parts, helping them blow their noses when snot was running down their faces, and helping them use the restroom. That's how disabled they were.

Caretaking became full time jobs for us, on top of school and chores. Every day we had to get wood chopped, stacked, and brought into the house for the fireplace. In the summertime we had to keep the blackberries down and the poison oak cut back. It was always a lot of hard work.

I also worked on a farm right up the road from my grandparents' house, taking care of five horses, two dogs, five cats, and four goats twice a day. The owners were truck drivers and were never home. I liked that job because it got me out of my grandparents' house and gave me breaks from in-home care work with my family, which was a lot to deal with for a young kid from the streets of Southern California.

Chapter 4

Before we moved north, I was held back from the second grade due to a lack of attendance. That meant that I was a grade behind everyone else when I moved in with my grandparents. I struggled with the realization of knowing less while being older than all the other kids in my classes.

Nothing I did ever seemed to be enough, no matter how hard I studied or how much time I spent on assignments. I never got the good grades I desired. I wanted to be an A+ student but mostly had to settle with passing grades throughout grade school and high school.

I did excel at PE and music classes. I played bass guitar and was on the basketball team every year. Even though I was technically in Special Ed, I still did well in those fun classes.

I had friends my own age in the upper grades, but whenever I was in groups with them, I'd become a laughingstock—the easy one to pick on. I never really knew how to defend myself verbally and always resorted to getting physical. As a result of that, I developed some anger problems early on.

In high school I had anger management classes and counseling twice a week up to the age of fifteen or sixteen. They helped me learn how to deal with my anger, where it came from, and how to fix problems thoughtfully.

It's taken years, thirty-six years actually, to completely gain control over those emotions and impulses. But now it really takes a whole lot to get me mad. In fact, I've learned that I can't be mad at anyone else but myself for allowing negative things to happen in my life. I can choose to stay and feed into the problems or simply walk away and never look back at them.

I had to learn how to deal with my own issues and experiences, discarding what wasn't needed and holding on to the things I cared about. For me, that mostly meant bikes, fishing, basketball, music, and love.

It's actually a miracle that I'm even still alive. Growing up the way I did made me very mature in some ways. In a relatively short amount of time, I've encountered just about every negative thing a human being could come up against in an entire lifetime.

Chapter 5

I've always loved water. When we were young, my mom would sometimes sneak us kids into a motel that had a swimming pool. One of the memories I have of my dad was at one of those pools. He'd pick me up over his head and throw me into the deep end. I guess that was his way of trying to teach me how to swim.

As I got older, I'd sink to the bottom of the pool by letting the air out of my lungs, and then time myself to see how long I could stay underwater. I remember wishing I could just live down there.

While at the bottom, I always thought the light shining through the water above me was the most beautiful thing ever. I felt like I was one with the pool. When I swam, I would glide through the water with little resistance, then pop up out onto the edge of the pool, kind of like Free Willy.

When I lived at my grandparents', the Van Duzen River ran right behind our house. It was just a five-minute hike to the water. There was a deep swimming hole down there with a rock cliff we could dive off.

One hot July day when my brother, sister, and I got home from summer school, we immediately changed our clothes and made our way down to the river. At the bottom of the hill there were about thirty steps that were really small and steep. I had run up and down those steps thousands of times. That time I decided to try to hop over one of the steps, skipping it completely, but I lost my balance.

I started to fall forward while trying to slow myself down. I was basically running down the stairs and I kind of fell off the cliff at the

bottom, right onto a pointy rock about five feet from the water's edge. It took a huge chunk out of my knee. I struggled back to the house. My grandma had to rush me to the hospital about thirty minutes away for stitches.

After my accident, my grandma started taking us kids to a less dangerous place to swim called Rainbow Bridge. It was a popular spot to pull off the main road and go swimming. Oftentimes there would be other families down there swimming too.

One day us kids were down there swimming. We had our goggles and snorkels and were diving down under the rapids. We could see all the baby salmon smolts that had hatched the previous winter. They were three to six inches long. There was a giant stump with roots that the fish liked to hide under.

All of a sudden, I heard screaming and splashing. Not fifteen feet away from me was a little girl, four or five years old, and she was being swept down the rapids. It was obvious she didn't know how to swim. Without thinking, I swam as fast as I could and pulled her back to safety. Her parents thanked me for saving her life. It didn't really seem like I'd done anything special—it was just instinctual for me to help her. I was probably twelve at the time.

When I was in the seventh or eighth grade, I had to pick a Friday elective. The options were art, cooking, music, chess, math, pottery, or triathlon class. I chose triathlon.

We had to practice swimming, biking, and running. We trained at the College of the Redwoods, outside Eureka, every Friday for upcoming races. There was one triathlon called the Foggy Bottom Milk Run, and another at the college where schools from around the county competed. You'd get out the water, swim laps, run a couple miles, then hop on a bike and ride ten plus miles. I was pretty fast back then and came in second place in one of the races. I was in good condition from living in the mountains.

Chapter 6

As far back as I can remember, music has been a huge part of my life, including songs my parents listened to when I was in the womb. The very first song I remember hearing is "Angel Baby" by Rosie and the Originals. It's an old '60s song and has a kind of haunting quality to it. That song is a part of my mind as if I listened to it every day.

I remember after we moved to my grandparents' house, when I was still a little kid, I'd listen to the radio and wait for my favorite songs to play, hoping every time a new song would come on that it would be one that I loved. I'd lay on the floor, trying to send telepathic messages to the DJ at the radio station so he'd play my favorite songs.

As I grew older I always tried to stay up on new music as it dropped, keeping a playlist of all my favorite songs. Back when CDs were still cool, I'd spend all my money collecting them so I could play whatever I wanted to hear on my five-disc CD player. Now everyone can just listen to any song they want, whenever they want to, on the internet, but when I was younger you still had to scrimp and save to be able to afford to listen to your favorite music.

Chapter 7

Feeling lost so much of the time led me to being curious about drugs. At the age of fifteen, smoking weed seemed like it fixed all my problems. Growing up in the woods of Humboldt County, marijuana was everywhere. I figured it wouldn't be there if I wasn't supposed to smoke it, so I did, just like everyone else.

Early on I was something of an outcast because I didn't smoke weed. Due to peer pressure though, and the availability of the product, I not only started smoking, I eventually became a weed dealer at the age of sixteen.

It began with just trim, then bud, and before long I was making oil and setting up hundred-pound deals for all the pot growers I knew. I became a middleman, talking with people from all over the country, connecting the dots and trying to build business relationships. I was spending all my time working for the growers and out-of-town people, but somehow I wasn't getting paid much for my time.

I had two phones and was nonstop setting up deals and trying to get everyone on the same page. I was having to build trust between growers and dealers, hoping each would stick to their word and show up on time to complete the transactions.

I loved that job and I did it, off and on, for over ten years, making everyone else happy and rich. But in the end, I had nothing to show for it besides knowing the right people. I got to thinking I should move away, meet some new clients, build some new business relationships, and expand my clientele. With all the new dispensaries

opening up in California and Oregon and everywhere, you couldn't beat the weed business. It could be very good money if you knew the right people.

At seventeen, I dropped out of school and moved out of my grandparents' house. They didn't want me around anymore because they thought I was going to get in trouble with the law. Over time I pretty much lost touch with my whole family and was just totally on my own. I stayed at friends' houses and continued selling weed to high school students and people around town. I became known as the weed man. When I ran out of money, I'd buy a $100 garbage bag of bud trim and turn it out with a system that would yield me $6,000 to $8,000 in return. Now, I'd tell you how I did that, but you know I'd have to kill you, right?

Chapter 8

I paused my drug dealing somewhat when I turned eighteen and decided to join the California Conservation Corps. The CCC protects, preserves, and rehabilitates the land and ecosystems that surround the communities we live in, as well as wildlife and forests in our national parks. It was a three-year program and just about anyone could join if they were eighteen to twenty-four years old.

The crews were very diverse. I made lots of friends from all over the country. Everyone tried to work equally hard to complete the jobs. If someone was falling behind, say, while we were hiking through the mountains, we'd all stop and wait for that person to catch up. No one got left behind and we all learned very quickly how to support each other to work as one.

We were sent hundreds of miles from the nearest hospital or even cell phone service, and our only way out to get help was by hiking long distances to get back to the trucks. Because of that we were very careful to avoid creating any emergencies. That brought the crew together even more and really taught each of us how to respect everyone else's space.

We all had our own problems and things going on in our lives that no one else knew about. We were working in the mountains with fifteen others who were tired, in pain, and often just completely exhausted. Sometimes our patience would wear thin. But you had to be respectful of the others and allow them their space. That was a valuable lesson I learned while working at CCC and it helped later when I was living in homeless camps, jails, and other situations like that.

There were five different crews, each one specialized in a particular type of job. My crew did trail construction and maintenance. We'd hike out to remote places in national parks and build new trails—cut away trees, remove stumps, and carve pathways into the sides of mountains. Everyone carried a full tool set with them that consisted of a Pulaski (a combination tool with an axe and an adze), a pickaxe, jack hammer, a small wedge, a large wedge, and all of our PPE (personal protective equipment).

I was a sawyer, which meant I was chainsaw certified, so I also carried a chainsaw. If we were working in a national forest, we'd have to use a whipsaw instead of gas-powered chainsaws. A whipsaw is one of those old-fashioned blades that two people push and pull. You can't use gas-powered saws in national forests because of the exhaust from the gas motors.

My favorite days were when we worked in the old growth forests, sitting down for lunch on a freshly built trail. The smell of fresh dirt and sweat meant to me that our hard work made it so people, for hundreds of years, could enjoy the trails we were making. Looking up into the canopy of those giant redwoods was just amazing. If you haven't seen them, I recommend you do.

Another crew specialized in invasive plant removal. They'd spend their days at the beach, pulling out beach grass and Scotch broom—those two non-native plants were from Europe. They brought them over here to help hold down the dunes and keep the wind from blowing sand up onto the railroads, but now those two plants outgrow all the other vegetation, killing many native plants.

The third crew, salmon restoration projects (SRP), traveled to large creeks to do their work. The mountain headwaters once had many creeks that held salmon and steelhead trout for thousands of years but are now blocked up with debris, mud, trees, and pollution.

The SRP crew's job was to go in and clear out those log jams using grip hoists, cables, and pulley systems.

After cleaning out the creeks they'd create a fish habitat by anchoring dead trees to live ones on the bank. They'd drill through both trees and slam inch-thick rebar through them, then they'd attach giant washers and nuts to hold the dead trees in place. They'd crisscross another tree over the first tree, half in the water and half out. After repeating that process two or more times, it would create one solid unit that would rise and fall with the water level of the creek. With that structure the water would naturally dig out a deep hole underneath and create salmon spawning pools. It was cold working in those creeks, but so beautiful.

The fourth crew was a fire/flood emergency response crew. They'd assist with handing out sack lunches, sandbags, and water, and setting up garbage, recycling, and whatever else was needed during or after large-scale emergencies, including forest fires, which happened all the time.

The fifth crew stayed at the center, fixed things, maintained vehicles, and sharpened tools. They were the warehouse workers. The center housed maybe 150 people. We had four people in a room, three meals a day, school at night, and we were paid minimum wage. Back then, that was $7.25 an hour.

Chapter 9

I spent three years at the CCC before joining the Backcountry Trails Program, which involved working for five-and-a-half months in the Stanislaus Mountains east of Stockton. There were fifteen to eighteen other crew members, and we were hiking five to ten miles every day. At camp we'd have nice, big meals waiting for us when we got home from work every day. The food was brought in on mules once a week and packed with dry ice to last until the next load arrived.

Our cook had been a chef for the Grateful Dead years before, and he made really good food. We were out the whole time in the Sierras without visiting any stores or having interactions with any human beings other than ourselves and the few hikers we ran into on the trails.

I was lucky because my girlfriend at the time, Megan, had been on the same crew as me the year before. I was eighteen when we met and she was thirty-six. She was familiar with the land and how the whole program worked. Megan would come visit me once a month. I felt like a king out there when she'd show up because I was one of very few of us who were lucky enough to have a visitor.

Megan spoiled me with plenty of love and support. We'd take off on the weekends and hike to her favorite lakes in the Stanislaus National Forest. There were crystal clear granite lakes up there, so clear you could see all the trout swimming around on the bottoms.

One of my favorite lakes was at the top of Granite Dome at 10,882 feet. When we were there, I felt like I was on top of the world. I was totally happy with just my woman, my fishing pole, our tent (which we only used if it rained), and two sleeping bags. We'd zip the bags together so we could make love and keep warm, while laying out under the stars. The stars looked so close at that elevation it was like watching fireworks. They seemed so close you'd almost think you were on the moon.

Chapter 10

After finishing the Backcountry Trails Program, I saved up all my paychecks and Megan and I moved into a place together, a one-bedroom house in Rio Dell. It was the first place I'd ever rented. I had enough for the deposit, first and last months' rent, and a couple of extra months paid in advance. I was hoping to find a full-time job so I could stay there for a long time.

At some point, Megan went off to a training program to become a horse farrier. A farrier is a person who trims and cleans horse hoofs and then nails on horseshoes. It's rare to have a female with those skills. Her business took off, but at the same time we slowly separated.

I was working for Labor Ready, a temp agency, hoping to land a full-time job, but I could never find one. After a while, working only a couple days a week wasn't enough to keep up on all the payments. Megan was damn near moved out by then and not helping with the rent at all. After a while I lost Megan and my place. I was fucked.

Laura, the mother of my best friend Tyler from high school, said I could stay at their house until I saved up enough for a new place. I was still working for Labor Ready in Eureka, and I was able to get rides into town with Mark, Tyler's dad.

Laura loved me as if I were her own. Sometimes it almost seemed like she loved me more than Tyler. I think that pissed him off. Laura used to grab me and hug me as hard as she could and not let go, kissing my cheeks. She was happy to have me staying there with them.

I wanted my own car to drive myself to work and go to other places. Mark was a mechanic for a used car lot called Roy's. He said there was a car there for sale that was cheap but would last me a while. Laura wanted to help me out and said to Mark, "Isn't it time to upgrade the backyard?"

Mark said, "Yeah, but if we're going to do that, we should upgrade everything—a new deck, sod, and garden."

Laura added, "I want raised planter beds, all the weeds dug up, and new plants and trees."

They asked me to do the work and in exchange they'd buy me that car at the lot, which would be my first, a '94 T-Bird LX. I jumped right on it. We agreed that all the supplies would be dropped off at the house and any tools I needed I'd get from the rental place. As soon as I could, I started digging.

First, I dug up the whole backyard about four inches down, making sure to get all the roots and weeds out so they wouldn't grow back. The whole backyard was full of weeds about three feet tall, the ones that have stickers and get stuck in your socks. I probably hauled a couple of dozen wheelbarrows full of dirt and weeds out of there and Mark took them to the dump.

The backyard was probably thirty by thirty feet. After I was down to bare soil, I put in raised planter beds all along the back side of the fence. I made them out of railroad ties, three high for each bed. I drilled holes into them and hammered rebar through and into the ground, about a foot down, to hold them in place. I had to take into consideration the amount of soil that was going to fill the planter beds, that's why I made the raised beds with such solid walls. I then had three truckloads of soil dropped off and I wheelbarrowed it all to the back of the house. I filled the planter beds, added bags of compost, and mixed it all together. At that point I was ready for Laura to go shopping and pick out all the flowers, trees, and garden ornaments.

Laura also wanted a small pond that had its own pump and lights that shined on a miniature waterfall. We got some solar garden lights to go all around the yard too. She picked out fifty different plants, shrubs, and trees, then placed them according to where she wanted them. I followed her and planted them all in the ground.

My project was beginning to look like one of Martha Stewart's backyards, like a picture in one of those magazines. I was feeling pretty good about the job I was doing. The last step was laying out the sod. I measured the yard and told Laura and Mark how much I needed. The next day a truck delivered it. I cut it and laid it out. Everything was looking good. Laura was in love with her new back-yard. I finished the job in about three weeks, and Mark brought me my car like he said he would. I was so happy. I worked hard for that T-Bird. I told myself, "I'm going to take care of this car forever."

Chapter 11

I started driving to work and feeling pretty good about how I'd taken care of myself by making responsible decisions. I was about to turn twenty-one. It had been a week since I got my car. Megan called me and wanted to throw a party for my birthday at a friend's house in the next town over. She said, "You have a car now, so bring all your friends, and I'll bring all my friends in my car."

I was like, "For sure."

It seemed like she wanted to get back together. At that point I was really missing her and wished we could figure things out. I felt jealous, and thought she'd probably met some cowboy while horse-shoeing and that's why we'd broken up.

Everyone met up at this farmhouse owned by one of my friends. We had half gallons of whiskey, vodka, and tequila, which was my favorite. We were all drinking and having a blast. At about 3 AM, Megan and I started fighting. I could have sworn she was flirting with one of my homies and I got pretty angry about that. So she said, "I'm leaving."

"No, you're not."

I was totally shitfaced, but she'd stopped drinking hours before and was almost sober. Megan tried to leave, and I tried to stop her. We were yelling and arguing. She got into her truck and drove away. I figured I'd just follow her, but I started looking all over for my keys and couldn't find them anywhere. I was tearing up the house and nobody was helping me look for them. It turned out Megan had hidden my keys from me earlier in the night and told all my friends not to tell me where they were while I was still drunk.

I finally found the keys behind one of the rear back tires. I jumped in the car and took off looking for Megan. I was still drunk. I don't know how I made it to the next town without driving off Fernbridge. That bridge is really long and narrow. It was built in the early 1900s, and the Eel River runs underneath it.

I made it to Fortuna. All I remember was making a right turn by the park and then all of a sudden BAM! I'd looked down at my radio for a second and somehow veered off to the right, just enough to drive under the bumper of a huge, parked truck, totaling the right front of my car.

The next thing I knew, I was being tested by the cops to see if I was under the influence. They got me at twice the legal limit. I was once again fucked. I'd only had my car for a week and then, on top of losing my place and not being able to find a full-time job, I had to pay for DUI classes and get my car fixed. The relationship was also definitely over with Megan at that point.

Chapter 12

I wanted to find a job where I could use the skills I'd learned while working for the California Conservation Corps and the Backcountry Trails Program. The only thing I could find was working for a fire/water restoration company called New Life Service Co. It wasn't working in a forest, but it was still a very good job with room to advance, which I did.

We'd go in and clean out fire burned or flooded houses, then remodel them from the ground up. I started as a laborer hired on through Labor Ready, then after a few months the company hired me on as a painter, then about six months later I became an asbestos abatement supervisor.

At some point around then, I started going to this little bar called The Shanty every day after work. I made friends there and would play ping-pong until 2 or 3 AM, and then wake up with a hangover before going off to work. I was trying not to let my boss or the other crew members see the addiction that had begun taking over my life.

I had started using cocaine. I had a rare connection because it was hard to get coke in that neck of the woods back then. I started selling it to all my friends at the bar. It was good, fast money on top of the $18 an hour I was getting paid at my job.

Around that time, I also met a few different girls that loved to party. We had the time of our lives using coke, whippets, alcohol, meth. You name it, we tried it, except for heroin. When I was a kid, my parents were always shooting up, so the sight of hypodermic needles made me feel sick.

Back to the good part of the story—the girls I would bring home were sexy and full of curiosity in bed. Doing coke and drinking with them was one of the best times of my life. But at some point, I brought home two girls in one night. Let's just say that was the beginning of the end.

I began missing work—partying was so much more fun—and I was making more money from selling drugs than I was at my job. So, I quit, like a dumbass, and slowly fell off. Soon I lost my place, my car, and all the hot girls, and ended up homeless on the streets of Eureka. That city is probably one of the worst places in the country to be homeless too. There were very few resources, only a couple of places to eat, and a lot of careless people committing all types of crimes.

Chapter 13

The basic survival methods of living on the streets, while being exposed to the elements twenty-four-seven and having to make quick decisions always kept me alert. I was like a wild animal. I had to keep my head up, stay strong, and never let my guard down, or show any signs of weakness.

Living that way caused me to become emotionally sensitized to every living thing around me. Animals and plants were fine, but finding people to trust was the hardest part of the lifestyle. Locating just one other person who could potentially become your partner, your mate, the closest person to you, was very difficult. It's hard to come across someone like that at all, and even harder to do while you're trying to survive on the streets.

I spent a lot of time by myself. I found it much easier to overcome obstacles and distractions that way. The bottom line was that it wasn't worth investing time in someone who was just trying to get over on you the first chance they got, while taking advantage of your feelings and emotions.

I found that the longer I lived outdoors, homeless, the more I was pulled down even further into chaos. It made every day seem even more impossible to find the light at the end of the tunnel. That light just got smaller and smaller. The more I tried to reach for it, the faster it would fade.

It was very hard to fit in with society. People living the homeless life are looked down on by everyone. I know there are a lot of people struggling all over the world with homelessness. No one seems to know how to fix the problem. I can see the destruction it brings to communities and individuals in society. For some, it's a choice to be homeless. There are a lot of people out there who are basically good but just fell down the wrong path, stemming from a lack of parenting, structure, and support.

Maybe those people didn't have the right kind of discipline as kids or maybe they never had anyone to love them unconditionally growing up. That can lead you astray from the common ways of living a normal life. But I believe with enough support anyone can change. Some people just need a hand up instead of being pushed aside for someone else to deal with.

That's why I always tried to help the people around me on the streets. I tried to raise their spirits and convince them not to give up. I wanted to become a living example, to show that anyone can overcome the worst in life and still make it to the top! Or maybe not the top, but let's just say make it a little ways up from the bottom, which can feel like the top once you've been down for so long.

Society makes it known that the homeless need to stay at the bottom and are not worth investing any time in. I don't know if it's the smoke that saturates our clothes, or our calloused hands with dirt filling the cracks screaming for soap and lotion, or maybe it's our dirty fingernails that set us apart. It could be the hand-me-down clothes we wear from free boxes and donations from shelters.

How about when we hoard too much stuff or supplies, like stock-piling goods, building materials, electronics, toys, bikes, cars, you name it? That does look pretty bad from the outside, but when you're in survival mode you never know what you, or someone else, might need at any moment.

Perhaps it's that we can be seen riding on an old bike, or riding a bike while ghost riding another one (taking it some place to repair or use for spare parts), or how about pulling a huge cart full of a bunch of different bikes while riding a bike that's the wrong size for us? I've been there, and I guess I can understand how that might set us a little apart from the rest of society.

Let's not forget the way people stare at us all through the store the whole time while we're trying to shop, waiting for us to steal something. My anxiety would make it nearly impossible to shop at Goodwill because I didn't like that feeling at all. I'd just be in and out, trying not to draw any more attention to myself than there already was. It seemed like I was always being watched, twenty-four seven, always under attack in one way or another.

/ Chapter 14

One day I met this chick, Sophie. She was not my type at all. I figured maybe I'd just get high with her and have sex and leave, but she had other plans. Before I knew it, two and a half years had gone by and we were living day to day in a rundown motel, hustling to make the rent.

We were always fighting. Sophie was really negative about everything I said. After a year I figured out why. She was going into the bathroom, shooting heroin, and keeping me from knowing. Sophie knew how much I hated heroin addicts, because of watching my parents shoot up as a kid, and finding needles all over the house. I remember getting poked by a needle that was left on the couch when I was five or six years old.

Everyone who lived at the motel was a part of some type of drug activity. One day the cops came and raided the whole place. There was a warrant out on me for some minor stuff I hadn't taken care of, so technically I was on the run. They busted into our room, cuffed me, and took me off to jail. I was in custody for two weeks. That was the first time I'd been incarcerated for longer than a day or two at a time. I couldn't wait to get out.

When they finally released me, I caught a bus back to the motel. Sophie had boosted me all kinds of stuff—clothes, shoes, a Bluetooth speaker, and a bunch of cans of Dust-Off, which has always been my favorite drug. She really knew how to spoil me, to make me want to stay with her.

I saw everything laid out on the bed, all the gifts and everything, and the first thing I did was grab a can of Dust-Off and begin to get high. Sophie had the bubble full of meth. She'd gotten some weed and alcohol too. As I began to hit the bubble and pop a bottle of Corona, she asked me if I was ready for my other gift. Surprised, I said, "Yeah, what is it?"

Sophie told me to lay down on the bed and then she began to slowly take off all of my clothes. As she kissed my body, she took my arms and legs and tied each one to the bedposts. Then she blind-folded me as I was lying there completely naked, sprawled out on the bed.

She said she was going to fulfill all my fantasies. She took her time slowly licking me from my neck down to my, yep, you guessed it. She teased me for what seemed like hours, getting me all the way there, ready for release, then she'd stop and start all over until I couldn't take it anymore.

Sophie rubbed me down with baby oil and then put it all over her breasts. She started sliding up and down my whole body. Then she dripped hot candle wax on my chest. She untied me and then I flipped her over and got on top. We did it for hours—that was the most exciting experience I'd ever had with Sophie, that's for sure.

Afterward, I sat on the edge of the bed thinking to myself, "What can I possibly do to never end up in jail again?"

I'd just had the time of my life and never wanted to risk losing my chance of doing something like that again. I was thinking there had to be something I could do to make money that didn't involve continuing to sell drugs and risking my freedom. I began to con-sider how I could not only change my life and my way of thinking, but how maybe I could help others at the same time.

If I was going to help fix anyone else's problems, I needed to be able to communicate with them. I realized that most of our prob-lems in life lead back to communication itself. Second, I thought to

DUST
Off

myself, "Maybe I can use the internet, like creating an app or even a website?"

I came up with the idea to build a social network to help spread knowledge all over the world. I wanted to bring people together to talk about their questions about life. I envisioned the main page of my website with a globe of the planet earth just spinning and spinning around, but I never got around to actually making it happen.

Chapter 15

I ended up eventually leaving Sophie and the motel and moving into a tent on the beach behind the Bayshore Mall. There was a homeless encampment there and lots of other people hanging out. Everyone was boosting stuff from the nearby Walmart, and I was trading drugs with them for the stuff they stole. They were taking food, flashlights, clothes, sleeping bags, tents, and all the other things you need to survive outdoors like that.

I was tweaking at the time, so I rarely ate but when I did it was something quick and easy. I used to buy hot dogs that I could cook on a campfire. I also bought jugs of water, then I'd fill up the empty containers at a spigot down the trail by a Porta-potty. When I went in to buy anything, the Walmart people always followed me around. I think that store is closed down now because they lost so much money from all the theft.

I started finding lots of cool rocks on the beach and collecting them. I piled them up around my tent and various other places around the encampment. There were all different kinds of rocks: green ones, red ones, some of them seemed to be made partly of gold. They could have traveled a long way to get to that beach, who knows where from. There were always new rocks showing up all the time. I wanted to try to melt down the rocks with the gold in them, but I never got that far.

I went through spiritual attacks there and got messages from God. I'd stay up all night reading the Bible in my tent. I went through various mental tests. Everyone else out there seemed to be going

through similar things, but some people couldn't handle it. There was one guy who damn near tore his ear off because he was hearing things. It was like we were all going through spiritual warfare, and only some of us came out safely on the other side.

Chapter 16

When I was twenty-five, God began to lead me away from Eureka and that tight-knit little community hidden away from the rest of the world. Surrounded by redwood trees, rugged coastlines, and long mountain ranges there were very few roads connecting it to other towns. Highway 101 was the one main road into and out of the city. It was an ideal place in some ways, but I wanted to get away from my homeless lifestyle there.

I thought I'd travel north and see where it took me. With nothing to lose, I set off hitchhiking. I made it to the next town, Arcata, which was about a twenty-five-minute drive away. Arcata was known for being the location of Humboldt State University, and for having lots of hippies everywhere, always smoking pot.

There was a square in the middle of the town called the plaza where all the hippie kid travelers united in a giant 4:20 smoke-out every day. You could find just about any kind of drug you wanted there—mushrooms, acid, coke—you name it. All you had to do was be patient and chill on the plaza, which was surrounded by bars and clubs on all four sides, and the drugs would come to you.

There was always something poppin' on the plaza and when there wasn't, it was because the cops were close by, or had just been there, trying to catch someone committing an illegal offense or getting into a bar fight.

I kicked it there on the streets hoping to find someone heading north to hitch a ride with. After a few days, I met a whole school bus full of hippie travelers. They said I could go with them when they were leaving town. I felt thankful—I could finally move on from Humboldt County, where I'd been living for almost the last twenty years.

I was so ready for a change. I couldn't wait to experience something new, see new territory, meet new kinds of people, and just find out where life was going to take me.

I had no money. I felt like a bum. But I fit right in with those hippie kids in the school bus—all dirty, dreads, smelling like B.O., talking crazy slow. I'd damn near fall asleep trying to have a conversation with one of them. Not to hate on those kids, I was in the same position—lost, looking for a way out, and stoned most of the time.

The next day, the owner of the bus said we were ready to go and that everyone had to meet up at a certain time. I came to find out that all the hippie kids were out spanging (panhandling) and trying to sell everything they had to get enough money to fill the gas tank. I asked how much they needed to get on the road, and the bus owner said something like $200 to fill the tank of that gigantic vessel.

The bus was a diesel and a gas guzzler. My first thought was, "Great, we're never leaving now, and if we do, how far will we get?" I was still like, "There is no way anyone is going to give that much money away."

But to my surprise, people do that every day. Those hippies had been spanging since they'd started the trip, way down in Southern California. I was amazed.

We finally left with a full tank of fuel. But guess how far it got us? Only just past the Oregon border, which was like, two-and-a-half hours from where we'd just left. We broke down at a casino in Gold Beach, Oregon.

I thought to myself, "I can't spange, I can't ask people for money like that, it's embarrassing."

I had too much respect for myself and the people leaving the casino. More than likely, most of those people had already lost all their money. I thought I could probably travel a lot further and faster if I hitchhiked alone, so I left the hippies and their school bus and continued on by myself.

Chapter 17

I walked down Highway 101, got a few hundred yards, and came upon a Native guy drinking Watermelon Four Lokos, a malt liquor that's like 12 percent alcohol. It's kind of an energy malt liquor drink. The Native guy was already plastered. He offered me one of his Four Lokos. There were four more unopened cans in his bag. I thought, "Hell, I'll drink one," but one led to a few, and in a short time we were both wasted.

It was about to get dark. The Native guy offered to let me go back to his house on the reservation. I agreed, not really having any other plans at that moment. We started walking back to his house when, all of a sudden, I woke up lying in the middle of the road on a side street.

I asked, "What happened?"

The Native guy said, "I don't know, you were walking forward, then fell onto your back."

I'd busted my skull on the ground, split my head right open. There was blood everywhere. I had a concussion. Everything was blurry, not to mention I was still faded from the alcohol, so I didn't remember anything. I thought maybe I'd been shot from behind. The hole in the top of my head was the size of a fifty-cent piece. I couldn't understand how falling down had put a hole in the top of my head like that. The Native guy went to his house, got me a towel, and told me to go to the hospital. I didn't know where the hospital was, or even where I was for that matter.

So, I just continued to walk north on 101. Nobody would pick me up in the dark in the middle of nowhere with blood all over me. As I was walking, I came into a little town. I can't remember what it was called. I found a spot to lay down and rest in the tree line across from a Safeway.

Finally, morning came. I was really hungover and didn't know what was going on. Everything was a blur for about the next three months. I barely remember anything from that time. I slept in the tree line for a good three days before I had the energy to hitchhike again. I don't think I ate or drank anything at all that whole time.

I walked and walked, probably ten miles before I finally got a ride to Eugene, Oregon. The driver dropped me off at a shelter and I was able to get some food and water. But then I was stuck in Eugene for over a week living with the other homeless people, trying to figure a way out of town to the next city.

Chapter 18

I met this older man, a drunk who was a train hopper. We started drinking together one morning. Both of us got wasted, and he suggested we hop on the next train coming through town headed to Portland.

I said, "That sounds like a hell of a good idea, let's go. Let's get the hell out of here, anything to get out of this fuckin' place."

I'd never jumped onto a moving train before. The man said, "It's not going to stop—we have to hop on as it slows down passing through town."

I heard the train coming. The horns were blaring, letting us know it was getting close. We waited for an empty boxcar with its doors open. Finally, our chance arrived. We ran alongside the train while throwing our bags into the boxcar, then we made an extended leap up onto the train, pulling each other up. We were both laughing, saying to each other that we'd made it. Even though we were drunk already, we continued the party, popping another tall can and sitting back to enjoy the ride.

Later on that night, we reached Portland. It was my first time there. I didn't know how the city was laid out. I didn't know north from south. I didn't know where we were going to jump off.

We had to make sure we didn't go too far into the train yard because we could be arrested and charged with a federal offense. We got off right by the Steel Bridge, both still drunk, and began walking around aimlessly.

I asked the old man, "What do we do now?"

"I don't know."

We walked around for a couple more hours before deciding to hop the next train going back down to Eugene. I didn't like the idea of going backwards, but I was unprepared for a big city like that all of a sudden. It had been a spur of the moment idea, but at least I then had the knowledge about how to hitch a ride on a train.

We jumped on the next train headed south and, in a few hours, we were back in Eugene. I thought to myself, "What the hell am I doing, I was there in Portland, why didn't I stay?"

The very next morning I decided to hop another train by myself back to Portland. I figured since I was no longer totally drunk, I could find my way around better. I got on the next train that came through town. I started to get comfortable. I was a little nervous but felt pretty good about doing everything on my own.

I ended up falling asleep. I woke up and the train was blaring its horn as we were pulling into Portland. I got ready to exit, but to my surprise the train didn't slow down one bit.

I began to wonder why the train wasn't doing the same thing as the one we had been on the night before. It actually seemed to be speeding up and switching tracks. The train began heading east and was moving way too fast to jump from. I was stuck on that train and didn't know where it was taking me. My worst fear was that it was traveling all the way back east and might never stop. I didn't want to leave the West Coast.

Eventually, after a long time, the train finally stopped in a place called Fairfield, Oregon. I was in the middle of nowhere, in a very small town. I didn't want to try to take another train, so the only way back was a Greyhound bus. I had to ask a church to help me with food and water because I had no money. I told the pastor I'd been hitchhiking and fell asleep and wound up going past my destination. I told him that if they could help me get back to where I'd come from, it would be a miracle and blessing. They bought me a bus ticket, and that's how I found myself once again heading to Portland.

Chapter 19

As the Greyhound bus pulled into the station in downtown Portland, I was getting nervous thinking about what might be around the next corner. I figured there had to be a reason why I was there. Exiting the bus my first thought was, "Where do I go from here? I don't know north from south. I'm totally lost and turned around."

While traveling I always paid close attention to directions. I figured if I ever got lost, I could head south and eventually find my way back home to Humboldt County. But at that point I had no idea which direction was which. I decided to just follow the homeless people scattered throughout the streets. Finally, I reached the Steel Bridge on the waterfront. It was a nice sunny day. I laid my blanket out on the grass and took a nap. When I woke up, I thought to myself, "What the hell am I doing so far from home?"

I didn't know where to go. I was surrounded by all kinds of new people. Some of them seemed crazy, some just freaky-scary. I remember being so nervous that I had butterflies in my stomach. I really wished I could just be back in Humboldt County. I fell asleep again.

Waking up that evening on the grass at the waterfront, I realized I was starving. I started asking the homeless people I saw where I could get some food and shelter. They all pointed me in the same direction.

I wound up at the Portland Rescue Mission and was not impressed with it at all. There were people laying all up and down the sidewalks rolling in filth, food, and spit. There were crazy people yelling and fighting. I was like, "No way this is really happening to me."

I waited in line, finally got some food, then asked for a couple of wool blankets. I was not about to sleep there with all those dirty people. I figured I'd go back to the spot I'd napped at, on the grass by the river. I was hoping nobody would mess with me, and the cops wouldn't arrest me. Being new to town, I probably stuck out like a sore thumb. Throughout the night I had to get up two or three times to move due to sprinklers going off and soaking me.

Chapter 20

Morning came and I was woken up by police telling me, "Move on, you can't be sleeping on the waterfront from 10 PM till 8 AM," or something like that.

I stashed my blankets in a bush and went exploring. I wanted to see what this new adventure had in store for me. I retraced my steps to the shelter and was able to grab breakfast and find out what time lunch was. Talking to other homeless people, I was able to find out where I could get help with resources and where to go for food stamps.

I knew with a food stamp card I could get $200 in food right away. In the past I'd had to pull that hustle just to get some money in my pocket. I could sell my $200 in food stamps to just about anyone for $100 in cash. I figured I could flip that $100 in cash by buying and selling some drugs and double or triple my money, or I could buy a bus ticket to the next city, which was Seattle, Washington. I made the decision to keep going.

I found someone to buy my food stamp card, and I turned around and bought a Greyhound ticket to Seattle. As the bus pulled out of the station, I kept wondering why I'd been in Portland—there had to be a reason, something drew me to that place.

Having never traveled before, I was beginning to like my new freedom: freedom to wander anywhere without ties, with no one telling me where or how to live my life. It felt really good making my own moves and plans.

After I arrived in Seattle, I did the same thing I'd done in Portland. I found the shelters for food and information as soon as I got there. I realized people were not as nice and conversational as the ones in Portland, and nowhere near like the people back home in Humboldt. The people in Seattle were all cracked out, literally. All the homeless there were just like the crackheads you see on *Cops*.

I did my best to stay away from the bad parts of town. I'd begin my days taking public transit everywhere it was free downtown, just riding back and forth sightseeing. Seattle and Portland are both really pretty cities, especially after coming from the dark woods of Humboldt County.

Even during the worst and most confusing times, it was still the most freedom I'd ever experienced, and I wanted more. After a few months, winter was setting in. I wasn't liking the idea of being stuck out in the cold and snow. I didn't want to sleep in the shelter with the crazy, ruthless homeless either. The few times I did that, I got bitten by bedbugs and swelled all up. I was allergic to the bites.

Chapter 21

One afternoon I went to a church where they were feeding the homeless, the Church of Jubilee. That was where I really came to understand how powerful God is, and how much he was trying to save me and lead me in the right direction. That's where I had another run in with the Holy Spirit within myself.

It felt so good during the church service, I began to break down and cry. I couldn't stop crying. The music they were playing hit me so hard. "Come as You Are" was the name of the song they were playing.

At the service the pastor was teaching us how to forgive, and so in my mind I began to forgive. First up were my parents for not being there all my life. I'd been mad at them since I was a kid, but I knew that was just my excuse for everything being so fucked up in my life. When I started to forgive, my mind began to lighten up, the heavy weight on my shoulders went away.

It was around October and the weather in Seattle was getting colder and rainier, which was forcing me indoors at a shelter. I didn't want to sleep in a place with bedbugs, on a mat with one wool blanket on the floor two feet apart from over sixty other men. The smell alone would drive any sane person away from such a place. That's not including the danger and risk of getting into a confrontation with a crazy or a drunk or a crackhead. Every night, those Seattle shelters become a "safe haven" to any person living on the streets, but those places were far from really being safe.

I heard the news of some homeless people dying because of the cold weather and decided to search for a halfway house or a church residential program of some kind. I found a discipleship in Tacoma that would accept me into their program. They normally only took in men who were court ordered after being released from jail. I was the only one who voluntarily joined the program.

What an impact that decision made on me. I knew I was on the right track, finally. That was where I fully realized that I was on a spiritual journey and, yes, God was leading the way. That was where I began to pay a lot more attention to the signs around me in my everyday life. I learned to slow down enough to recognize all the different ways God was trying to communicate with me. I started coming to the realization that He had a whole world of living color to use to try and lead me out of the dark, and into His light.

After about two weeks in the discipleship, even though I was developing a lot of insights, I had to excuse myself. I was getting bitten all up by bedbugs. Seattle has a bad infestation of those nasty, creepy bugs. If you've never seen one, they look like a tick but about three times smaller. You can't feel them crawl on you, and they only come out of hiding to feed on human blood. They are as nasty as they sound. I couldn't take it anymore, so I had to leave.

I caught a bus back to downtown Seattle to a resource shelter. I found info on other places to live, but none of them would accept me right away. Eventually though, I did find a job as a carny for the Davis Show fair and carnival. They just had a few weeks left in the season. I thought to myself, "Hell, I may as well work, get paid, and sleep in a tent with the other crew members while traveling around with them."

I got the job right away. I started in the food truck making elephant ears all day. I didn't like that very much. It was hot from the fryer and always busy. I wanted to run a game or ride, and after the first week or so I got to do that.

It was an experience I'll never forget: all the sounds of kids screaming with joy and laughter, the rides spinning, the lights flashing, the customers shouting when they won, and the smell of cotton candy, popcorn, and corn dogs. Even after we were shut down for the night, you could still hear all the noises in your head. It was a fun, exciting job, and we got to travel around a little, so it worked out pretty good for me.

Chapter 22

After the season ended I'd saved enough to pay for a week in a motel. I wanted to quickly figure out what to do next, and I did. One of the halfway houses I'd previously contacted emailed me back and told me there was a bed open. The house was part of the United Way and was located just outside of downtown Seattle.

The requirement for living there was that each day we, a van full of dudes, would be driven out and dropped off in rich neighborhoods where we would then solicit door to door. We were supposed to ask for donations, not only to help get us back on the right path as individuals, but also to support the cost-of-living expenses for running the whole house. It was a nonprofit organization type program.

I'd never done that kind of work before and I hated every minute of it. About half of the people we talked to would offer their support, but first you had to basically grovel and sell yourself, which is the part I didn't like, convincing the homeowners that they were donating their money to a worthy cause. On a good day, I'd bring back $200 or $300, but it was a painful process.

Chapter 23

My roommate and I decided to save our money and fly to Hawaii where it was warm year-round. My roommate had been there before and was familiar with Honolulu. Me on the other hand, I'd never been on a plane in my life and had only traveled around the West Coast—California, Oregon, and Washington.

We bought our tickets a month in advance and barely had enough to pay for the flights. I knew when we got there we'd be sleeping on the beach until we were able to find a place. We were both totally broke when we landed. I had some food stamps, but that was about it.

Our plan was to get up early every morning and go to Labor Ready. We did concrete work, roofing—any kind of manual labor jobs. That worked out. We got paid enough to make it through the day and afford alcoholic drinks and *pakalolo,* which is weed in the Hawaiian language.

I also posted "labor for hire" on Craigslist every day. At some point we got a hit back. An old lady and her mom needed help moving their house down to Waikiki from the North Shore. After getting to know those two old ladies while assisting them for a week of loading and unloading, they were nice enough to help us get an apartment right next door to them. They knew the owners of the building who let us move in with what money we had made by helping the ladies.

It was perfect. We went from staying on the beach to living in an apartment within two weeks. We were sleeping on blow-up air mattresses on the floor. We had a radio and a fan. The rest of the apartment was empty. It was OK because when we weren't working, we were at the beach getting drunk and enjoying ourselves—living the high life.

We'd hang out in Waikiki, probably the most recognized tourist area in Honolulu, with all these college kids. We fit right in, except when we'd pass out drunk and wake up hungover and half-conscious, and everyone else would already be long gone. Eventually, we'd stumble back to the apartment.

After about two weeks we both got full-time jobs working for a sign company called Creative Signs. They started us out at $14 an hour and made me an installer. The signs we worked on were lightboxes out in front of various stores. Part of my job was driving around the island checking on the various signs, making sure they still worked and installing new ones. It was like a dream come true. Everything was working out just as we'd planned.

I was there for about a year. My buddy only stayed six months because we had a fight one night. He was drunk and tried to bully me around. I knocked the shit out of him. I think he felt so bad he just decided to go back to the mainland. I stayed and continued to work.

I didn't know how long I was going to be able to keep the place by myself. After a while I began feeling alone and really far from home. I started talking to this woman, Brandy, who I'd met online. She was from Salem, Oregon. We connected on Facebook through a high school friend.

We talked and talked every day, two or three or maybe even four hours a day, for six months, until one day Brandy offered to buy me a plane ticket to come stay with her. I was like, "OK, let's continue the journey and see where it goes next."

I went to get on the plane. When I was in the security line, I remembered that my backpack, with all my stuff, including my ID, had been stolen. I hadn't replaced anything because I'd found out

it would take months to get a new Social Security card and a birth certificate. Without those things I couldn't file for a new ID card.

The people at the gate said they could run my name in the system to verify who I was and then I'd be able to continue onto the flight. When they ran my name, a warrant popped up. It was from right after we'd first arrived on the island. I'd received a ticket for sleeping on the beach and never went to court to take care of it. That eventually turned into a warrant for my arrest, I just hadn't realized it.

They called the cops who, when they got there, took me straight to jail. I went to court the next day and had to pay a fine. Once that was all worked out, Brandy bought another ticket. I was able to pass through security without an ID card. It was a hassle, but eventually it all worked out.I found myself on a plane back to the West Coast to meet a woman I'd talked to for six months without ever having met in person.

Chapter 24

For the first three weeks we were fucking like rabbits, and everything was great. Then my life took a sharp turn. The absolute opposite thing I was prepared to have happen, happened—Brandy got pregnant.

I was shocked to hear that I was going to be a father. Being a parent was one of my life goals, but I wanted it to happen when I was ready, not all of a sudden like that. Nevertheless, I immediately wanted to create a perfect life for my child. I didn't want him or her to grow up like I had, without a real father.

In the beginning of the relationship all was going well, but I soon realized Brandy and I didn't see eye to eye on most things. I was only twenty-five years old. Things were moving way too fast. I was still trying to be a hustler, a baller, a player. I wanted to make my millions and retire at a young age. That was my mindset, at least.

We began getting into arguments, then fights. Brandy was carrying my first child, so I never wanted to put stress on her and the baby. We'd both lived hellish lives in the past, we had that in common. But we'd lived through our own individual versions of hell, and as a result we had our own unique ways of managing life. That created friction and communication problems for us.

When we'd start to fight, I'd take off and go drink beers away from the house, down by the river, until I was drunk. Then I'd go back and make up with Brandy, but the next day would turn out the same way again. I knew it was not healthy for either of us.

That carried on for a couple months until it got to a point that I just left, not for good—just for a while. I was hoping a little space might make things go better between us.

I went back to California. I didn't want to go but I had to. I didn't want to put her through any more stress. It really bothered me, leaving during her pregnancy. While I was away, I stayed in touch and checked on her until the baby was born. We ended up having a son.

Chapter 25

I traveled back up north to Salem to try to make things work out for our new family. But things didn't really change. I started to feel like Brandy had just used me as a sperm donor. After all those months with her, I found out she already had three other kids, each from a different dad. None of the kids were in her custody. Her family took care of them. They were all under seven years old.

Not knowing what to do, I just tried to stay close. I began living the homeless life in Salem, hoping to figure out a way to be in my son's life. I immediately went looking for a job. I put in applications everywhere. I went to a temp agency. They helped me get work at the Coffin Butte Landfill in Corvallis, picking up plastic and non-biodegradable trash. Brandy was driving me to the job site and then picking me up. Gas was burning up all my money. I was only getting paid sixty to seventy bucks a day, and that went quickly. After three weeks, I knew I needed to get a job closer to Salem.

I found one at a Walmart in Albany, Oregon. I was hired as a laborer on the construction crew and helped build the store building. When it was done, Walmart hired me as a stocker and warehouse worker. I'd never worked in a retail situation before. It was an easy job, but dealing with customers all day was not much fun. Wearing the blue vest and singing the Walmart cheer every morning sucked too.

After about three months, I couldn't stand it anymore. I needed something better that paid more than minimum wage. I went back to the temp agency. They helped me get another job working for

WinCo as a night stocker, which meant I didn't have to deal with customers anymore. Besides that, the only real difference between Walmart and WinCo was that WinCo had slightly better benefits, slightly higher pay, and I didn't have to wear the vest or do the cheer anymore.

But things never improved with Brandy, so eventually I quit my job and moved back up to Portland.

Chapter 26

I wanted to stay in Oregon to be near my son. To do that, I survived on the streets of Portland as a homeless person for ten years. That was the most confusing, depressing, stressful, lost, unbelievably lonely time of my life. I tried to keep a positive mindset, and I knew if I trusted and believed in God and His word, He'd never lead me into any situation I couldn't handle. I had to be there in Portland for a reason. It was part of God's plan.

I spent those years searching for answers. I wandered around, literally every day, wondering what life had in store for me, where God was leading me and why. I tried to be open-minded and gave myself plenty of time to figure things out. I avoided certain people and attempted to keep others close, people who I knew were on the same level of understanding as me. I worked as hard as I could. I was always trying to better my life in any way, but with little support or guidance.

It's very easy to give up and say fuck it when you've lost everything, such as your family, your kids, your jobs, your house, and so on. It's much easier to just be high so you can avoid thinking about the pain. I'm not saying I didn't enjoy getting high, because I very much enjoyed getting high, and in many ways even thrived in some ways during that time. It's just also a way of not having to deal with everything that had gone wrong in my life.

I actually kind of lived like a king on the streets. I loved the freedom of working for myself and being needed by the people around me. I always kept a lot of items for trade or sale that people used to survive, like tents, sleeping bags, bikes, inner tubes, patches, phones, socks, men's and women's shoes and clothes, food of all sorts, bottled water, feminine products, condoms, cleaning towels, even clean needles. I kept stock of just about everything, including, of course, drugs.

I became the go-to guy for many people on the street. Every day, I'd have close to twenty or thirty people come by my spot for one thing or another. It felt really good to be able to help others in that way.

I built relationships with almost everyone out there—some crazies, others who were just lost like me. The only difference between me and them was that I had instructions from God. I needed to teach the people His word and lead them in the right direction in life.

I became kind of a street counselor and something of an advocate for the people I served. I'd spend time talking to various folks trying to give them positive reinforcement that things would soon be getting better. I told them that they had some very valuable tools given to them from God. That would give them energy and lift their spirits before they ventured back out into the streets of Portland. My spot became a sanctuary, a safe place away from the rest of the world.

I had to lead by example the best I could. I know I'm not a saint, but I did try to be the most respected man in my own society, even while living in a tent.

Chapter 27

At some point I met Sarah. She was also homeless and had been for years. She was mad at the world, a very angry person. She'd lost her kids and was struggling with life. I tried to help her get out of that funk and back on the right track. We were homeless together living by the Steel Bridge.

The city's Rapid Response Team started pushing everyone out of downtown, and they threw away all our stuff. There was nowhere to move to at first. Sarah was Native and some people from the Native American Rehabilitation Association helped us move into an apartment, right off Southeast Grand Avenue. It was a one-bedroom place, and they helped us with furniture and everything we needed. It was a pretty amazing deal—free rent for life—as long as we didn't fuck things up.

Sarah got a puppy from somewhere, a Pomchi (a Pomeranian-Chihuahua mix). We decided to name her Cleopatra because she was like royalty. Her hair was wavy golden. Everywhere I went, I'd take her with me. I put a basket and a blanket for her on the front of my bike, and I'd go out on long bike rides with her through the city and out into Oaks Bottom on the bike path. I'd bring along my Bluetooth speaker and blast my music, mostly rap and hip-hop, which Cleopatra seemed to really enjoy. I remember looking down on her hair blowing in the wind.

One day we were cruising in the bike lane. I had Cleopatra snugged into my backpack. I could hear a train a ways away. I started pedaling as fast as I could to get across the tracks ahead of us before the arm went down to stop traffic. Right before we got to the tracks, we were passing a line of cars that had stopped. Then, a guy in one of the cars opened his driver's door and we slammed into it. I took most of the impact, but it threw us ten feet forward into the street. Amazingly, Cleopatra was OK, just a little shaken up. I was mostly alright too, but my bike had a bent front wheel, so I ended up walking home.

At some point, Sarah got aggressive with me, and we had an argument. I pushed her off me. She called the cops, and I got arrested. I had all kinds of bikes and other stuff in that apartment that I was fixing up and using for trade. Sarah let everyone we knew into the apartment while I was in jail and they took all of it. Then Sarah got herself thrown out of the apartment for breaking various rules, including letting all of those people inside the apartment.

When I got out of jail, three weeks later, I had to just start up again on my own. Sarah was not in the right state of mind to take responsibility for Cleopatra. I'd always taken care of her anyway, feeding her and walking her and all that.

We kind of had joint custody. When I'd wind up going to jail for a few days, which only happened four or five times, or took off on a trip to California or something, Sarah would take care of the dog. Once I'd get back and settled in again, I'd find out where Sarah was staying and go get Cleopatra.

Cleopatra lived with me for over five years off and on, and then Sarah gave her to this guy named David. He's a really nice guy who always minded his own business, but Sarah didn't ask my permission when she gave Cleopatra to him, so that was a little upsetting. It might have been for the best though. Cleopatra always really liked David, and I was here in prison anyway and wouldn't have been able to take care of her.

Cleopatra was like an emotional support animal, and not just for me and Sarah—everyone she met loved her.

Chapter 28

I paid my way for everything. All the neighborhood shop owners knew me well and greeted me when I entered their stores. They'd say they loved it when I came through because I always brought them business. I enjoyed spending my money in those stores because everything I purchased was for survival—my own and the people I resold the stuff to.

I made my money in a few different ways. Number one, I'd trade dope for aluminum cans—about fifteen to twenty black garbage bags each day. Then, I'd go cash the bags in, making about $20 from each. I'd make about $200 to $300 every day just on cans.

The canners wanted dope for their cans, so it was pure profit for me. I'd pay them like a pinch of dope per bag, which was just a point or two on the scale. For that price, I could buy myself a lot of bags of cans and everyone was happy.

I know selling drugs was not ultimately helping anyone out in the long run, but people were going to spend their money anyway, if not with me then with someone else. Selling to me got them a lot more than just their drugs. It gave them someone to trust and go to whenever they needed to talk or get support.

During the COVID-19 pandemic, when stores stopped taking in cans, business skyrocketed for me.

My number two way of making money was selling bikes, phones, speakers, tools, jewelry, gift cards, you name it. Boosters would bring all sorts of products to me to trade for dope, then I'd turn around and trade or sell what I got for either more dope or money.

That was every day, all day and all night. Being in that position made me feel important and filled my empty, lost, confused spaces with some moral sense of what life was all about.

Chapter 29

After being released from jail for something minor one time, I returned to my spot to find that all my bikes had been stolen. I walked around to all the people I'd known to see who might've taken them. To my surprise, I could not find one. I thought to myself, "They must've hidden them from me, knowing I would be on foot looking for them."

I tried to borrow a bike from some of those so-called friends of mine, but nobody would loan me one, which made me assume everyone was in on it. We're talking about five to ten bikes, vanished. Nice bikes, too.

My personal bike, the one I rode everywhere, was a full suspension Trek with 29-inch tires that I bought from Goodwill for $200. All the other bikes I had were brought to me in exchange for drugs. To my knowledge, very few of them were hot.

When people brought me the bikes, I'd look them up on the Project 529 website to see if they were stolen or not registered. If they weren't registered, I'd register them in my name, then I'd resell them. The hot ones, I'd get rid of as fast as I could. I had a guy for that. He'd buy the expensive ones from me, no questions asked.

Bicycle cops were always stopping by to run my bikes through the system. Most people actually thought the police were part of some kind of bike theft scheme themselves.

One time, a cop took my Trek and I had to wait three months for him to wrap up his investigation to see if it was stolen. Finally, he confirmed that it hadn't been, but then I had to go pick up the bike at the police warehouse. It was huge and packed full of bikes of every kind. It makes you wonder what they do with all those unclaimed bikes, doesn't it?

Back to the story. I was walking around for days, looking for a bike to ride, and none of the people I knew had a working bike they would let me borrow. I even tried to put together a bike made out of all different parts, spray painted ten different colors, but I couldn't get it to work.

I needed a bike bad. I had a court date. I needed to go shopping for food and to ride to go take a shower. Plus, I needed transportation out of the area in case of an emergency. When you're living the homeless lifestyle, your bike is essential, like your phone or even your shoes. Without shoes, you're not going anywhere, and same with a bike.

I was getting tired of walking all the time. It had been three or four days since I'd been out of jail, and my feet were killing me.

I was walking back to my spot when I saw this bike. It had a full suspension and was locked to a stop sign by First Avenue and Salmon Street. There was a bar or a brewery on the opposite corner and a restaurant with giant windows and tables outside on the other. My spot was only a block or two away. I said to myself, "Oh, damn. I'm going to steal this bike."

It was attached to the pole with a small cable and a combination lock. I went to go get my bolt cutters. I returned five minutes later to steal my first bike. Honestly, that was the first time I ever attempted anything like that.

I walked up and pulled out the bolt cutters. I went to cut the cable and as I pressed down, the lock just popped open. I hadn't even cut the cable yet. The bike was dummy locked. I figured that the lock must have been broken, and the owner had just made it look like it was secured.

I put the cutters back into my backpack and unwrapped the cable. It was broad daylight, people were everywhere, cars driving back and forth. I went to hop on the bike to race off, but the bike was stuck in first gear. I couldn't get the thing to shift. I was just pedaling super fast while trying to get away very slowly.

My legs were moving enough to be running, but the bike was only moving like one mile per hour. It was ridiculous. I could have walked faster than the bike was going. Everybody who saw me stealing the bike was probably laughing their asses off, watching me trying to flee like that.

I got off the bike and walked it a couple blocks to Morrison Street. I was thinking I'd made it out of there safe. All of a sudden, five or six cop cars pulled up on me. They arrested me and took me back to the station, questioning me the whole time about being part of some organized bike theft gang. They thought I was one of the ring leaders. I told them I wasn't, that I just bought random bikes from people on the street, but I wasn't a bike thief. I explained to them that it was the first bike I'd ever tried to steal. All the cops in the room started laughing. They said if that was the case that my luck was not very good, and neither were my bike theft skills.

While still laughing, they informed me that the bike had been rigged and that's why I couldn't shift the gears. It was a bait bike, and they had me on camera from the start. By then, I was laughing myself. I could only imagine what I must have looked like trying to get away with the bike. I never tried to steal another bike again.

Chapter 30

For the first three of those ten years on the streets in Portland, I camped out in a tent. After dealing with wet and cold weather through a few winters, I got smart and built a portable box on wheels to live in. I started with a six-foot cart for moving pallets and heavy loads. I then found a big pallet and laid it down evenly centered on the cart. That was my base to build up from. I framed out a box with two-by-fours. The walls were five feet tall, and the base was ten feet long in both directions.

I took plywood and nailed it up to the frame, leaving a three-foot door for an entrance at one end. I covered the box with thick tarps, which held heat in and kept me dry. It was big enough to fit a twin-sized mattress and two people—me and a girlfriend—comfortably.

I cut a queen-sized memory foam mattress in half and placed it on top of the twin-sized mattress. That bed was really comfortable. It had down blankets and hella pillows that I'd scavenged. Someone had dropped their used bedding off on the sidewalk, but it was all basically brand new. That was one of those times I wished certain items would show up, and sure enough, God provided for me once again.

The box was my safe place, my hideout away from the world, my place of privacy. I used it to escape the crazy world outside. That lasted a couple of years before I realized I could build an even larger portable tiny home.

I found a pop-up trailer from the '70s that no one wanted. The tarped canopy on top was rotting away so I gutted the whole thing,

took everything out, and just left the metal frame box trailer. I built it all out so that the space was about ten feet tall, eight feet wide, and about twelve feet long with a pitched roof made out of clear plexiglass. I'd found large sheets of plex, overlapped them, and heated the center to make a V-shape for the roof. It deflected the rain, but I still had sunlight, and natural heat.

I insulated the walls and made some shelves on the inside, which held my music playing devices. I turned the tiny home into a giant speaker box—the whole thing would vibrate. It was like being inside a giant house speaker. I'd lock myself inside and then turn the music up as loud as I wanted.

That tiny home was the first of its kind in my neighborhood. Everyone wanted to see the inside and it inspired others to try to build similar ones. It was much better than sleeping on the ground or in a tent. I lived in that place for about three more years before someone burnt it down when I left town for a couple of days—haters.

After that, I moved into a fifth wheel that was twenty-seven feet long. When I found it, someone had dropped it off on the side of the road. It was still in good shape for the most part. It didn't leak water, and everything worked, but it was full of cobwebs, dust, trash, and bat poop. I cleaned everything out and began remodeling the inside, painting, caulking the cracks, sealing up any places the ants were coming or going. I put in new floors and then moved in furniture. That was a major upgrade from the tent and the tiny houses. I was a lot more comfortable and felt safer from the outside world and the weather.

But no matter what I did, people were not happy with my progress. The people around me began to plot and plan to overtake my new residence.

Let's just say my fifth wheel was burnt down to the ground by the same people I took care of every day, those very same people who I listened to every time they had problems—the ones who, when they were starving, I'd feed. When it was snowing outside and they had no jacket, I'd give them one. I'd go and spend money on those people no matter what, just to help them out. Those same people who, when they needed socks, shoes, clothes, hand warmers, a bike, I was there for them.

I gave those people blankets, water, batteries, propane, and flashlights. I gave the women feminine products when they needed them. Hell, I was always there, even just to provide positive encouragement at any time of the day and night.

But they burned down my homes anyway.

Chapter 31

The Portland streets taught me a lot. It was always a battle between the good forces and the evil forces out there. Growing up, I didn't really understand the difference between good and evil. I never experienced much good and was surrounded by evil, so I guess evil seemed like it was just normal.

The closer I got to God, the more beautiful the world began to look. That's when I'd stray off into my newfound world. I was living without a care, feeling untouchable at times, like I was already in the heavenly realm, as if I was invisible to the average human being.

I found peace and serenity, and the world I was living in was finally all mine. I was the creator. I could create things however I wanted them to be. That was the gift of being one with the Holy Spirit. Little did I realize it, but that beautiful world I thought I'd made was actually the same place I'd been born into with so much evil.

In 2012 I began hearing music differently. It never sounded so good. I could register every little beat and the vocals became clearer. Music began making more sense to me too. That's about the time when new artists just started falling out of the sky. The only way to keep up with all the new music coming out was to use the internet and Myspace and apps like Spotify and Audiomack.

I'd spend most of my days listening to music and saving songs I thought were going to make it to the top. Most importantly, some of the songs I was listening to seemed to reflect parts of my life. Most songs had subliminal messages that allowed me to connect with them. I almost felt as if I was the judge, picking which songs would become hits, especially with all the new artists producing so much music so fast.

I've always had an ear for what's hot. I'd go into the matrix, transported, traveling to another world and becoming one with the music. It was magical.

I started wondering to myself, "Could we humans communicate without words, just using sounds—beats, tones, tics, and knocks?"

Chapter 32

Moving from Humboldt to Portland, I really noticed a difference, especially in the people I encountered. Portland had weird and scary nights, and dark vibes that you'd get from complete strangers walking by with a smile on their face and an "I'ma kill you" look in their eyes. They had slow, fidgety movements and would appear out of nowhere talking gibberish or screaming at the air or somebody no one else could see.

In the spiritual world, I believe those people were actually communicating to someone on a whole other level—a far-off dimension or some portal or something. Even with all my experiences, I still found it interesting to learn where those people had come from and how they came to be in such strange forms.

That was just another example that let me see the difference between good and evil and how lost and bad life could really be. I had to be thankful for everything God had been teaching me while preparing me for what was taking place all around me.

I believe evil stems from a lack of knowledge and never really knowing what love is or feels like. Either way, good and evil can be used in the wrong way. Knowing that, you could use both to your advantage and potentially overcome evil and thrive with the good. That's becoming something greater than both good and evil. That's becoming one with the Holy Spirit, GOD HIMSELF.

Chapter 33

One morning I was woken up at the crack of dawn by a friend trying to trade me a car for an ounce of dope. I wiped my eyes, got out of bed, and told him I'd be out in a minute.

I stepped out to see a Mercedes-Benz G Wagon, all white, on 32s parked near my tent. My friend handed me the key. I opened the door to an all-white leather interior and tinted, bulletproof windows. It was a brand-new G ride—a stolen car.

My friend said he wanted to get rid of it before it was reported. He said he'd been walking around the night before and when he passed by the Benz he just decided to check the door. It was unlocked. He went through the car and found the key in the glove box.

He jumped in the driver's seat and went to pick up one of his homegirls. Then they just drove around all night. He said he only wanted an ounce of meth for it. I gave him what I had on me, which was only about half an ounce, but he took it. Then I went to go see what I could do with that $100,000 car.

The thing was that I didn't have anyone I could think of to take it off my hands for me, so I was like, "Fuck it, I'm gonna drive this thing back down to Humboldt."

In Humboldt, I could trade it for at least fifty pounds of pot, if not more. I could then sell the pot for cash and get back to Portland with hella money. I grabbed my backpack and threw some clothes in it. I had about $100 on me, and about $50 in recyclables, so I brought those with me too, then I hit the road.

First, I stopped in Salem to try to find my son and his mom. As soon as I got there, people were staring at me hard. Not only was my G ride exotic and sick as fuck, but when I got out of it, I didn't look like the kind of guy who owned a $100,000 car. I realized I had to get out of town and back on the freeway before someone reported me.

I kept the tinted windows all the way up and the music on high, bumping my favorite songs from my phone. It wasn't long before I came to the exit heading towards the coast and Humboldt County. I thought it'd be safer to stay off the main freeway. I was driving with the intent of getting to California as fast as I could, and the closer I got, the more excited I became and the faster I drove. I was using the whole road, passing cars on straightaways and taking advantage of the power that car had—it really handled the S turns.

I felt so comfortable driving that Mercedes, like it was made for me. I was coming around a corner before a giant straightaway, probably ten miles before Coos Bay, while listening to the AM radio about God. The sermon told me it was time to surrender to God's will and that it wouldn't be long before my life would do a complete turnaround. The preacher said I'd have to face my sins, accept them, and understand that it was only for the better.

Just as I heard that, I was thinking, "God, let me make it to California, then I'll be good."

Right after the corner, parked on the side of the road, was a highway patrol car. I flew past him, probably doing at least ninety miles an hour in a forty-five mile an hour zone.

The cop's lights went on and he pulled me over. I was like, "Fuck, here we go."

He walked up and asked me, "Do you know how fast you were going?"

"No."

"I clocked you going at least twice the speed limit, and I've had several reports of someone driving recklessly. Can you show me your license and registration?"

"I don't have any. I borrowed the car from a friend and was just trying to get home to California."

He went back to his car and ran the plates. The car was so new, it hadn't even been registered yet, so he came back and told me to turn off the engine and give him the keys.

I was like, "OK."

I rolled up the window and took off like a bat out of hell. The car was so fast, I lost the highway patrol car within seconds. I was gone. Little did I know there were two more highway patrol cars ahead, waiting to join the pursuit.

I had three cops behind me and I was passing cars though sharp S turns. It felt like I was in a *Need for Speed* PlayStation game. I remember flying across this long bridge and at the end there were cops on both sides of the road with spike strips. As I passed by them, I hit the spikes with my front left tire.

The chase was about over as I made a last sharp turn. The flat tire made me lose control and I drove into a curb. With eight or more cop cars surrounding me, I got out with my hands up. They arrested me and drove me all the way back to Roseburg, where I sat in jail for four or five days.

Amazingly, they let me out with a court date scheduled for months later. I couldn't stay in Roseburg for three or four months at a shelter. I didn't know anyone there. I had to figure a way out of town. I thought, "Should I go to Humboldt, or back to Portland?"

I chose Portland. I had no money so I asked people how I could find a ride back up north. The shelter I was staying at told me that the local Salvation Army gave out one-time vouchers for the Greyhound bus—one way wherever you want to go. I applied and they paid for my ticket. I made it back to Portland. I remember walking back to my spot and everyone questioning where I'd disappeared to for the last week. I said, "I went on a trip."

Chapter 34

During my thirty-six years of life, I've been tossed more than a few curve balls, and yet I've managed to overcome most of the obstacles I've encountered. But when the COVID-19 pandemic hit and the riots happened during the Black Lives Matter protests, Portland became a very scary place to live on the streets. I didn't really understand the meaning of the protests. On the streets there are no politics, it's just everyone for themselves.

When those riots started with thousands of people protesting, and when Trump first got elected, the streets turned into a free-for-all. It became an open market for just about anything anyone could get their hands on, stealing and causing destruction. Some people I knew were breaking front windows to jewelry shops, grabbing whatever they could, and jumping right back into the marching crowds.

Skateboard shops were getting broken into, too. It seemed like everyone I knew had new longboards or bikes. There were brand new items from all kinds of stores filling the streets, and if you were a dope dealer, you had any and everything you could want from trades—Bluetooth speakers, shoes, phones, clothes, tools, household items—and all brand new.

When the riots and lootings were taking place, I stayed out of the way and just watched from a distance. I'd never seen anything like it before. It seemed almost unbelievable. I'd see the drones and helicopters flying in the sky while watching their video feeds on the news at the same exact time.

My survival mode really kicked in when I started hearing rumors of martial law going into effect. It seemed like the whole world was ending, but I wasn't about to have my life taken away from me for some stupid reason or intentionally put myself into a position to have to worry about something like that. I was not going out that way.

In the back of my mind, I kept thinking about how hard I'd worked all my life. I wanted to be somebody worth remembering. There was so much I still wanted to do, so many things I hadn't experienced yet—most importantly being a real father to my son.

I thought about his safety and the safety of his mother. During those crazy times, I worried every moment. I was not around them and could hardly ever get ahold of them. The only reason I was still in Oregon was to be with my family, or what I hoped could be my family.

My gut feeling was telling me to leave town. Things were just continuing to get worse by the day and being already at the bottom, homeless, it was scary thinking that things could get even worse.

Chapter 35

Day after day passed, month by month, time began to fly by, and before I knew it years had drifted away. I didn't even realize my son had turned ten years old until sometime after his birthday. I told my friend I needed a vehicle. I wanted to get out of that fucked up place before something else bad happened to me.

Within days, he brought me a rent-a-car that someone had parked and left the keys in under the seat. The license plate was from Connecticut. It was a Ford Taurus hybrid plug-in gas and electric. I didn't have much money for gas, only forty bucks to see how far that would get me. I could also stop and charge the car at charging spots.

When I left, I grabbed a backpack with my most valuable things and a change of clothes, and I just bounced, leaving everything else behind. I kept thinking I needed to get out of town before it was too late.

All my money at the gas station only got me half a tank, but I had a full charge too. The car was telling me I had like three hundred plus miles of range. I was like, "Thank God, maybe I can finally make it all the way back to Humboldt."

I left town with no license, no money, no registration, and no real plan besides trying to find my son and Brandy. I was hoping that just maybe I could finally work things out with her and we could all get to safety together. She'd cut me off on Facebook a while before and I didn't have her phone number. I thought, "Well, maybe I can find the old street we used to live on."

I drove to Salem. I ended up finding the apartments we used to live in, but it turned out she'd moved. I drove around Salem looking for someone who might know Brandy or her mom. They were both well-known around town.

After a few days of driving around Salem, I figured I was beginning to stick out, especially with out-of-state license plates. So, I decided to just keep going south, not wanting to return to Portland. I took the on-ramp on Interstate 5. I was hoping by some miracle I could get some more gas and a charge, enough to make it to Humboldt County.

Whenever I'd see an electric car sign at an exit, I'd pull off for a couple hours and recharge the car. I don't know how, but I made it all the way to Crescent City, close to the California border. It was about 10 PM before I ran out of gas and electric power. I sold my Android phone to this kid for twenty bucks so I could get more gas. I was soon back on the road heading down Highway 101. It felt so good to make it out of Oregon. I began to see the redwood trees and knew I was close to home.

Around 2 AM I stopped at the Paul Bunyan Museum and checked my gauges. There wasn't going to be another gas station or power charging spot for over a hundred miles. I didn't want to run out of fuel and get stuck in the middle of nowhere along Highway 101. It was pretty dark along that stretch of road, with lots of cliffs and tight corners, and breaking down would not be a good option. I'd have to be towed or try to walk to the nearest town, and then I'd also be taking the risk that a highway patrol might pull over to try to help me.

I didn't have a lot of gas or power left, but I decided to go for it anyway. I figured I'd made it that far, maybe I could make it all the way. I drove through the rest of the night. By morning I was pulling back into familiar territory. I couldn't believe it.

There was just one big problem: everything was different—new buildings, new houses, the only thing that was the same was the jailhouse. I drove through Arcata, Eureka, and then to Rio Dell. I figured some of my old friends would still be around, and if not, maybe their parents could help me find them. It was 10 or 11 AM when the worst thing happened—I finally ran out of gas and power.

I pulled over and found myself in a residential neighborhood. I stopped in front of a house and couldn't go any further. The owner of the house came out and said, "What's the problem?"

I told him I'd run out of fuel. I apologized and said it wouldn't be long before I'd move the car. An hour passed. The old man came back out and asked if he went and bought some gas, would I hurry up and move my vehicle. I said, "That would be awesome, thank you."

He went and got the gas. When he came back, I tried to fit the nozzle of the can down the tiny hole into the gas tank, but I realized it wasn't working. I needed to make a funnel, but I didn't have anything to make one with. I was sweating at that point, trying to get out of the man's driveway before he called the cops. I was thinking to myself that I hadn't seen a cop yet on the whole trip and it was overdue for one to show up.

With my luck, a cop would come cruising up while I was fucking with the gas can. Sure enough, just as I finished spilling most of the gas all over the side of the car, out of the corner of my eye I saw a patrol car pull up behind me.

I don't know if the man had called the cops or not. I was only two seconds from driving off. A cop got out and asked me what the problem was. I said I'd run out of gas, but I told her that it was all good and I'd be gone in a second.

She went back to her car and waited for me to drive off. As I turned the car on, I looked in the rearview mirror just in time to see her lights go on—red, white, and blue. I was like, "No fucking way."

Long story short, she ran the plates and found out the car had been stolen from the state of Connecticut long before I'd gotten hold of it. They towed the car and took me to jail. I wasn't there for even a day when they let me out with a court date three or four months later.

Chapter 36

I found myself walking around Eureka in the middle of the night with no jacket or anything else. The first thing that came to mind was that I needed another car to get out of my stranded situation. Sad, I know, but I was out of answers and didn't know where to run to, or who to call for help. I was lost and freaked out. I honestly didn't know if I was going to make it to the next day.

Since that time, I've sometimes wondered what would've happened if I hadn't followed my gut instincts, and instead stayed in Portland, ignoring the signs that were telling me to leave town. Would I still be alive today? I felt like God was once again testing me to see if I could follow orders. He wanted to see if I was smart enough to escape my new challenge.

I remember it being so foggy that night it was damn near impossible to see anything. All my belongings were in the impounded car, and they wouldn't give them to me because I couldn't prove they were mine. I was totally out of ideas about what to do next. Everyone I knew had moved away, and my family didn't want anything to do with me, so there was no place for me to stay. I ended up at the only shelter in Eureka.

I had no food, no money, no bus tickets, no friends. I was stuck at the shelter. I was weak and tired, with very little energy, coming down hard off my meth addiction. All I wanted to do was sleep. I was stuck having to face the reality of starting all over again from the very bottom.

People take the simple things in life for granted. When you're trying to survive, making new friends is hard. You don't know who to trust. Not only that, but finding resources is a challenge. The first thing to do is figure out how to get food and water. Believe it or not, water is probably the hardest thing to find when you need it, and it's the most important.

Trying to find a hustle for some income or some government assistance like food stamps comes next. How about a voucher for clothes from the Salvation Army store? The clothes are never what you would normally wear. Same with the shoes. You wind up walking around town in brown khakis with a blue and orange striped long sleeve shirt that's a size too small, and someone else's hand-me-down shoes. It's a fucked-up feeling. It's so embarrassing because you're labeled right off the bat as homeless, which makes everything ten times harder. And good luck finding a job.

Four to five days had gone by sleeping at that shelter. I'd had enough of being kicked out at 5 AM, then having to be back around 7 AM for breakfast if I wanted to eat, just to be kicked back out again till around noon for lunch, then back out until dinner around 5 PM. After that I could maybe have a shower, but then it would be back into the line for a bed at 5 PM.

I'd be given a mat so I could share the floor with about seventy other homeless people. The smell in there was enough to make me gag. There were lots of people sick with COVID-19 and who knows what other kinds of diseases. That place was by far the worst I'd ever experienced.

I decided to find a tent and camp out in my old beach spot, behind the mall, right on Humboldt Bay. I don't think I mentioned it before, but that place was called the Devil's Playground. For having such a name, during the day the place was a real piece of heaven. At night though, it would come alive with spirits of the dead.

It was like having my own little beachfront property. The former encampment was gone, probably cleared out at some point, so no one else was around, and I had my own tiny place of peace away from the rest of the world.

Having something like that, homeless or not, helped me escape the reality of what was actually taking place on the streets. I felt free because no one was judging me. It was the place where my spiritual journey had originally begun. I'd spent many nights and days there reading the Bible and other spiritual and religious books. It's where I'd had many conversations with God.

I was back where I'd started. I kept wondering to myself, what's the reason for my return to the very same place I had been ten years before? Had I missed something the first time? Had I not completed my mission, or was I now supposed to realize something important that would be a key to fixing the destructive path I'd been on?

I spent a week camping out along the beach. The piles of rocks I'd made were still there, even after ten years. It was like nobody had been there since I'd left and everything had been put on pause while I was gone.

My piles of rocks were of every color. Beautiful rocks. I'd stashed rocks all over the place, so one day I'd be able to come back and admire them again. It seemed like each rock could tell a story. I loved spending hours combing the beach. I thought about building a public rock garden for others to enjoy too, but didn't make much progress on that.

The sun set in the afternoons with bright pink and orange clouds. They were so beautiful it felt like heaven. Man, I'd really missed that place where I had spent so much time before, but my gut began telling me to go back to Portland. I thought to myself, "I can't stay camping on this beach forever."

Everything had changed and no one I'd known was around anymore, except one guy I knew from before I'd left. He'd come down and visit me. We spent many hours on the beach having spiritual talks about God.

I started to contemplate a way out of Humboldt again. I knew the plan was going to involve a vehicle, and I was probably going to have to break the law—just one more time—and hopefully I could make it all the way back to Portland to recover whatever was left of my place if it hadn't been totally ransacked or burned down.

Chapter 37

One morning I woke up frozen and soaked from the condensation in the tiny tent I was sleeping in. I mean I was totally frozen—hypothermia was for sure about to kick in. I had to get out of there. I thought to myself, "I can't keep camping on this bay. It's wintertime and I'm not prepared for this weather."

I walked to a gas station all wet at about 6:30 AM. There wasn't much traffic yet. I had a blanket over me, but it wasn't doing much good. I needed to find some way to warm up.

Entering the store, the heat felt so good on my face and fingers. I had no money so I asked the person behind the counter if I could just grab a cup of hot water from next to the coffee machine. I explained I was freezing and really needed something to help me warm up. The attendant said no, that it would be twenty-five cents for a cup of warm water. I couldn't believe it. I went back outside and waited for someone to pull in to get gas so I could ask them for a quarter.

A white Ford truck pulled in and parked. The driver got out and headed inside for a cup of coffee. I asked him if he had a quarter, but he said, "No, leave me alone!"

He looked at me with disgust. I watched the man make his coffee through the window. He walked up to the counter and paid cash. I was like, "Fuck this place, fuck these people. How inconsiderate can they be? I can't even get a quarter for a cup of hot water!"

I was in a state of emergency and survival mode. As I was cursing the man who was buying his coffee, I realized he'd left his truck

running. My first thought was to jump in, that it was my ticket out of there, my sign to go. I actually didn't have another thought.

I ran over and got into the truck. I put it in drive and peeled off as the man ran out screaming and chasing after me on foot. As I cranked up the heat, I slowly began to thaw out, then I realized what I'd just done. I knew I had to make it out of town before the vehicle was reported stolen.

As I've said, there was only one main way into Eureka and one way out. But I also knew I couldn't make it far before the highway patrol would track me down if I stayed on Highway 101. So, I took Highway 36 all the way to Redding and over to Interstate 5 heading back north to Portland.

I made it all the way to Whiskeytown before two highway patrol cars went flying past me. I felt sure they were looking for me. I was being held up at a Caltrans construction site for like twenty minutes at the time. I said to myself, "Damn, that was a close call."

I watched in the rearview mirror to see if the cops flipped a bitch (made a U-turn) or not. But they just kept on going, thank God. I made it through the construction zone and into Redding.

I knew I was now in a lot better position on the interstate than I'd been on that two-lane highway. I could blend in with the other traffic. I kept pushing further north with just a quarter tank left. I was hoping to make it at least to Shasta.

I'd just entered the town of Weed when I ran out of diesel. I parked at a gas station and was trying to figure out what to do next. I was sitting there thinking, "Fuck, am I going to have to hitchhike from here, or should I sell one of the electric tools in the back of the truck to get some gas money?"

I looked in the rearview mirror and suddenly saw that there was a reserve diesel tank in the truck bed. I was like, "Oh my God, no way."

I got out and sure enough the tank was full. I flipped the on switch and began to pump my own fuel into the truck. I filled the tank and was back on the road. I drove all the way back to Portland nonstop. I couldn't believe I made it back. I felt bad for the man I'd "borrowed" the truck from, but I'd had to get out of that place before I froze to death.

Chapter 38

It was about 9 PM. I pulled into my parking spot around the corner from where my trailer was normally located. Everything had been cleared out, and a new trailer had been moved in. I knocked on the door and a man answered.

"What happened to the trailer that had been here just a couple of weeks ago?"

"Someone burned it down."

They'd ransacked my trailer, took everything worth any value, stole the mopeds I had out front and a bunch of bikes, and I'm sure they also stripped the two project cars I'd been working on for months. I guess that was my fault, for leaving everything behind like that.

I should've known that was going to happen, because they did the same thing the last time I tried to leave town. I just didn't know why they wanted to burn everything down too. After tearing through the trailer looking for valuables, the place probably looked like a tornado hit it, so it was probably just easier to burn it all down rather than get rid of the garbage no one wanted. I don't know.

I drove to some campsites around town asking people what had happened. Somehow nobody knew anything, but everyone had things of mine in their tents and trailers.

I was like, "Ok. Fuck it. I'm going to have to start all over."

Back to a tent! I'd worked my way out of a tent to various tiny homes, then to living in a couple of different trailers, and now I was walking around with just a backpack, one change of clothes, no money, no phone. Nothing. I thought to myself, "Why did I come back to Portland? Is this where I'm supposed to be? Do I really have to start over again with nothing? What is it that I'm not figuring it out, and why do I keep having to go through this kind of thing?"

At that point I felt very confused, lost, and afraid. I was also disappointed in myself and some of the decisions I'd made in the last few weeks.

Two days after getting back, I was still walking around pissed at how everything had played out—no home, back on the streets, walking around aimlessly. I was looking for some kind of sign as to where to go next. Again, I was wondering to myself, "Did I make the right decision coming back to Portland?"

One thing was for sure—I still needed to find my son. I had no idea where he was. That added even more stress, anxiety, and fear to my already freaked out state of mind.

On the third day, I met this guy while taking a break on the waterfront after walking all morning. He was a little younger than me. It was one of those random things, meeting someone for the first time and instantly finding yourself in deep conversation about the Lord.

We started talking about how unbelievable life can be, and that everything happens for a reason, even the randomness of two strangers running into each other at the same place, same time, going through the same life problems. Both of us had lost everything and were completely out of answers. Even though I'd been going through all of that, I still had the energy to try to help bring this stranger back up to a level of understanding of why things were, and how to overcome them.

I talked to that young man for about three hours, telling him how much God had affected me in so many ways. I tried to give him some insights into the journey I'd been on throughout my life. I gave him my time, not only to help through his struggles, but hoping maybe he could help me get some answers too. I continued to feel like everything I was going through was all part of a test from God—filled with fear, suffering, and frustration—to see if I was learning anything on my spiritual journey.

I invited that guy to come along with me, and not really knowing where we were going, he agreed. We stopped by a friend's camp, and he had two phones that I traded him for a little dope. As we continued to walk, the guy asked if he could use one of the phones. I was like, "Of course, and if you want to buy one of them just let me know, or maybe we could trade for something."

He said, "OK."

As we were walking, I noticed he had started to slip behind me about ten feet as we were making our way through town. That seemed strange, but I figured he would catch up. But when I turned around, the guy had totally run off with my phone. I was so pissed that we'd just spent hours connecting on such a deep spiritual level, and then he turned out to be a complete waste of my time and energy.

That was all I had left in my tank—I started to have a mental breakdown. I was so mad, so disappointed, and it felt like everything was for nothing.

I'd gone through so much loss at that point. I was on the verge of just saying, "Fuck it all. God, I'm so tired of trying, and every time I turn around, you're tearing me back down. God damn, how much more do you want from me? Haven't I suffered enough? Do you enjoy seeing me struggle? One human being can only take so much before they give in and just say fuck it!"

I was so pissed off at the world, and so afraid of what was going to happen next, I was walking down the sidewalk just cursing everyone and crying nonstop. That was the first time I'd ever cried for that long. I was emotionally and physically alone, ready to take out the world with a nuclear bomb. I was sitting behind a 7-Eleven bawling my eyes out, cursing everyone that passed by me. Even the people in

the cars driving by were pointing and staring. Some were laughing too. I never felt so low and embarrassed in my life.

I made a mental note about those cars going by me. It seemed like everyone in Portland was laughing at me, as if my life problems were being broadcast on the radio stations in their cars—"Look at that pathetic guy!"

So, I said to myself, "OK, you all think this is funny, I'm going to get myself a tow truck and tow your motherfucking vehicles so you can feel what it's like to walk around with nothing. And I bet when I do that, none of you will be laughing anymore."

Believe it or not, the next day I was walking to Target at about 5:30 PM when I came around a corner and there it was: a brand new F350 flatbed tow truck. As I walked by it, I realized the fucking truck was running. I looked at the business that the truck was parked in front of, and they transported exotic cars, but everyone had gone home.

The gate on the driveway was chained and locked and there was nobody for blocks. Nobody. I kept walking to the next corner and still there was no one around. I thought to myself, "No fucking way. I just said I needed a tow truck and here it is, and now I'm going to just keep walking?"

A voice in the back of my head said, "Fucking pussy."

So, I turned around and walked back to the truck. It was un-fucking-believable, but not surprising. How many of those kinds of things were going to just keep happening? I thought, "This is a blessing from God for sure."

As I walked up to the running truck I saw, in big-ass letters along the side, it read: "Enjoy the Ride!"

I was totally blown away. And I knew that nobody else except God was powerful enough to accomplish a thing like that. If it wasn't a perfect example of him being present in my life and looking out for me, then he was just showing off, especially when I'd been saying that I needed a tow truck just the day before.

I opened the driver's door and on the seat was a gas card and a box of business cards. I hopped in, put the truck in drive, and headed out around Portland looking for cars to tow. Driving down the road, people would look up at me and wave with a smile of kindness, or maybe it was fear. Driving around in that tow truck made me feel like I was in control of the road. People respected me, because I was driving a tow truck and could tow them at any time. They knew what I could do, and how much I could mess up their lives.

Well, it was fun while it lasted. The next day I wandered into Clackamas County and got lost in the cow fields. After driving around into the night, I nodded off for a second and drove through a fence into a pasture. Before I knew what happened, the cops showed up. I got hauled into jail for another UUV (unauthorized use of a vehicle). It was unclear to me if that was part of God's plan or not.

I was held, incarcerated at Clackamas County Jail for two days, and then let out with a court date in a month. In just a few months I'd racked up a total of four UUVs, all from different counties, each with court dates months apart.

There was no way I could make it to each county on time for hearings, especially without a vehicle. I wondered why they kept releasing me every time. I thought it was maybe a tactic for eventually putting me away for some considerable amount of time. For weeks, I tried to lay low and not draw too much attention to myself, while still trying to get a new vehicle for another run before I was caught.

Chapter 39

I didn't know where to go. I couldn't go back to California, or three counties in Oregon because of warrants. I thought maybe I'd try Washington State. Some might say I was going through a meth psychosis. I thought I was being followed, and it seemed like everyone knew what I was thinking.

I changed my plans throughout the day, five or ten times, never keeping to the same schedule, and whenever I got the gut feeling that the cops were getting close, I'd jump out of my tent and take off on my bike, riding as fast as I could around the waterfront bike trail. I'd make a giant loop going from the Steel Bridge to Tilikum Crossing and around again.

By the time I'd get back to the tent, everything would have changed. There would be a different energy in the air, almost as if I'd returned to a whole new dimension. It was a strange approach to problem solving, I know, but it seemed to work.

One morning I got up and someone had stolen my bike. I could no longer ride off and escape at the drop of a hat. I also began to wonder if that bike had a tracker on it, and if the cops were following me all around town trying to catch me.

I headed out on foot, walking from campsite to campsite looking for my bike. I ended up finding it down by the river, on a hillside in a homeless camp. I knew the chick that had stolen my bike: she'd been at my tent the night before mooching around, trying to get me to buy her alcohol, but I wouldn't. So, apparently, she'd come back later and stolen my bike.

I climbed down the hill to retrieve the bike, quietly because I didn't want to confront her yet. I didn't have time to argue with her because I needed to get moving and fast. I grabbed my bike, then climbed back to the top of the hill just in time to see the Portland Police driving hella slow, looking for something, possibly me. I figured they must have had a fucking tracker on my bike and were keeping an eye on where it wound up, then saw me walking around and searching for it. I assumed that was their tactic for trying to trap me. I jumped on my bike and took off, making my way around the waterfront, and losing the cops. It seemed like every time I eluded them, it just made them more and more pissed.

They began putting bait cars in the neighborhood that I camped in just to try to tempt me to make a mistake. I know I was not tripping. But in the back of my mind, I kept telling myself, "You're fucking tripping."

I was really going through it, not knowing who to trust, who was working with cops, where to run, what cars were bait cars, and what cars I was being blessed with when I needed them. It was like the other incidents where vehicles fell out of the sky. I didn't know what the fuck was what. I guess looking back, I was probably losing my mind.

Chapter 40

I was driving a Honda Civic. I'd gotten it from a friend and supposedly it was not stolen.

At some point I started being followed by a string of Dodge Chargers, each one a different color. It seemed like everywhere I went they'd follow me. Chargers were my favorite kind of car, and I wanted one so bad. Maybe I was manifesting them or maybe it was one of God's funny jokes he was playing on me, I don't know.

One night my dream came true. Just a few blocks away, I noticed a black Dodge Charger parked in the industrial area I was staying in after hours. Businesses had already closed up and everyone had gone home. The car was parked just in sight from my tent—three or four blocks away.

I was thinking, "That car should not be there."

I knew that nobody parked there normally. After spending so much time on the streets, you begin to notice patterns and certain times when cars leave or show up.

That Charger was totally out of place. I watched it for like four hours. Nobody came for it. I then began to wonder if it was my Charger, the one I'd been asking God for? Had he figured out a way to get the car of my dreams to me?

I decided to go check it out. Just maybe the keys were in the car and all I would have to do was open the car door and BAM, it'd be mine. I really thought that was going to be it. I'd finally have something I could call my own and ride off into the night with, never looking back.

I started to walk up to the car. I was about fifteen feet away from it when the headlights turned on. Then a Black dude got out of the car and said, "Almost."

I looked at him and replied, "Yeah, almost."

Then the guy did something I still can't believe. The lights were still on, the car was running, and he walked back behind the trunk, around to the sidewalk, whipped his thing out, and started pissing in the bushes.

Automatically, I reacted. I saw it as an open invitation to test drive my favorite car. I ran over, jumped in, threw the car into drive, and peeled off, leaving the guy standing there pissing. I never looked back.

I sped down to Salem again to try and locate my son, but once again, no luck. After driving around for a few hours, I was about out of gas. I turned around and drove as fast as I could back to Portland. As I looked over the hood of the car, I watched the reflectors and white lines zooming by. The faster I drove, the more traction I had, gripping the road so tightly.

That was freedom for me. I felt like I could drive like that every day for the rest of my life and never stop. With some music playing, I was in heaven. After being through so much negativity in life, that experience calmed me down. It gave me a sense of respect for the nicer things in my life, which I've always wanted so badly.

I parked the Charger not far from where I'd found it. Someone picked it up a little later. That was one of the funnest times I'd ever had in my life. It was such an adrenaline rush driving a hundred miles an hour late at night. Nobody else was on the freeway. It was just me and that giant motor.

Chapter 41

One week before being imprisoned, in the middle of the night, I was wandering around downtown Portland. I was driving an '86 Honda Civic. It was spray painted black, on its last legs, and looked like shit.

I met a girl, and we drove around all night, smoking dope and looking for a come up. We stopped every time we saw a free box hoping to find something cool and maybe worth selling. You never know, one man's garbage is another man's treasure.

I was hoping to get laid that night. I kept hinting at the subject. But she was more interested in getting high and had every excuse not to do anything else. As the sun was coming up, I gave up on the idea of having sex and turned to mentally preparing myself for the long day.

I stopped off at Home Depot to buy a can of Dust-Off, my drug of choice. With Dust-Off I was unstoppable, invincible. I could control all things around me after hitting the can. I connected a small, clear fish tank hose to the spray nozzle and ran it through the inside of my jacket so I could keep it in my pocket for periodic discreet inhales.

We were just sitting there in the Home Depot parking lot in that beat up Honda. I took a blast of the can and the WOMPWOMPS hit me. Then all the rainbow colors began to swirl as my vision blurred for a couple of minutes. My whole body got warm. I started tingling from head to toe. The sound of every living thing moving in the parking lot became one with me, like everything tuned into me.

As soon as my vision began to clear up, I looked in the rearview mirror and saw my black Charger on the other side of the parking lot.

Sitting there, while enjoying my high, I thought to myself, "That has to be the same Charger from my earlier test-drive. It had to have tracked me down, followed me all the way here to the Home Depot parking lot." I told the chick that was with me, "There's my Charger over there."

I started my engine and drove over to the Charger. I noticed temporary tags on the rear window and two Mexican guys sitting in the car with the windows up. Both of them were on their phones.

I kept looking over at them and then at the car, at them and to the car, back and forth. Then I pretended to get on my phone. I'd noticed that the guys looked nervous. Hitting the can I had tucked inside my jacket, anything and everything became possible. I was feeling good, damn near floating at that point.

In my mind I was thinking that I was just joking when I told the chick that it was my Charger. She looked at me and laughed, but I told her to roll down the window so I could get the attention of those guys.

They rolled their window down a little and looked scared and confused as to why I was interrupting whatever they were doing. Later, it dawned on me that they might have been in the middle of a deal. I smelled that something was not normal. So, I said, "That's a nice car."

They replied, "Yes."

I got out of my car and started walking around the Charger, noticing a few nicks and a crack on the dashboard. I looked through the window that was now rolled down all the way and asked them, "Where'd you get this vehicle?"

"Our boss loaned it to us."

"Well, I'm sorry but this is my car. It was stolen from me a few weeks ago. Call your boss and have him come down here to verify that this is his vehicle."

They called and we waited twenty minutes for someone to come, but nobody showed up. Keep in mind that I was still taking hits off the can. I was still floating and just kept going along with the joke. I couldn't believe those guys were going along with the idea of it actually being my car. I kept riding the wave out, not knowing how it was going to play out in the end, having never tried such a thing before.

I told the guys I had to go to work, and I couldn't wait around all day. Someone came and picked up the passenger, then there was only the driver left. I told him again that I had to go to work and that I wasn't leaving without my car.

I then asked him nicely, calmly, if he had any registration information that showed that the car was his boss's, and he said no. Apparently, there was no way to verify it was his. I said to him, "Give me the keys, I have to go."

"Can I grab my backpack in the backseat?"

"Yeah, go ahead."

He gave me the keys, and I told the chick to follow me. We jumped in, started the car up, and peeled off. Again, I could not believe what was happening. It couldn't have gone any smoother. It was like in a movie. It felt so good driving off in my dream car and leaving that junker Honda behind.

We drove around Portland all day sightseeing. We went wherever we wanted to. I ended up seeing a lot of places I'd never have seen otherwise, stuff you just don't encounter when you're homeless.

By the afternoon, I'd let the chick off somewhere and had ended up by the zoo. I was cruising around like I owned the car and lived in one of those nice houses up on the hillside overlooking Portland. As I drove down from the top of a hill, there was an explosion outside of the car—the tire blew. I overcorrected into the middle of the road. I was trying not to lose control and drive off into the houses to my right.

I skidded off into the bank on the opposite side of the road, hitting the hillside. My front wheels were in a ditch, just spinning. I couldn't get the car back out. Glass was everywhere. At first I didn't know what had happened or why. It was like someone blew up the car or shot out my tires. I didn't know what the fuck to think as I was standing outside the car with a surprised look on my face.

A truck just happened to pull up behind me with a winch. In a daze, I asked the dude to help me pull my car out of the ditch. But the dude's winch was not working. There were cars getting backed up on both lanes, all the way around the corner. People were recording videos with their phones, calling the cops, taking pictures. I was fucked!

I had to get out of there. I began walking down the road and then dipped off into the trees down the hillside, down to the freeway. I waited a couple of hours to be sure nobody was looking for me. I was shocked at how the day had gone, amazed actually. It was like I was in a movie that I hadn't signed up for! But I played the part well without having to read the script.

I waited till dark and walked back to town alongside the freeway. I was picked up by the police a few days later.

Chapter 42

I woke up around 7 AM on the corner of Southeast Second and Hawthorne. It was April 3, 2022. I didn't know it, but those were going to be my last few minutes before losing my freedom. I smoked a bowl as I attempted to regain consciousness, while trying to reflect on what my previous exploits might be bringing my way. "Oh yeah," I thought to myself, "I got a new work truck."

I had hooked up my friend with a Ford Ranger for a hella good deal months before. It was all legal. I didn't keep the truck because it was a stick shift. I prefer automatics.

That so-called friend had stopped by the previous night at about 11 PM and announced he had something for me. I said, "Oh yeah? What is it?"

"A completely legal work truck in exchange for the one you set me up with. It's a little beat up, but it runs."

"Sweet. Hell yeah! Where's it at?"

"Right down the road. But I need some gas money to take this girl to Astoria to turn herself in tomorrow morning. It's an emergency. Just give me whatever cash you have and we can figure the rest out later."

"I only have twenty bucks on me and a big bag of weed."

"Well, give me that for now."

"OK, hell yeah, that's a hella good deal."

I couldn't see the truck very well. It was spray-painted black. I noticed trash and leaves in the bed of the truck, spray cans, tarps. It looked like the truck had been sitting under a tree for at least a couple years. The interior was falling apart. It was probably a 1980 six-cylinder Dodge stick shift. My friend already knew I didn't like stick shift vehicles.

I thought it was very nice of him to bring me the truck but realizing it was a stick, I really didn't want it. I couldn't turn down such a good deal, though. So, I accepted the gift and asked him again if it was stolen. He said, "No!"

"Where'd you get it?"

"A friend owed me for a job and paid with the truck. My girlfriend and I ran the VIN number, and it's all good."

I took his word for it and gave him the only twenty bucks I had and the big bag of weed, which was probably worth about sixty bucks. There were at least four ounces of some good-looking weed in there, plus the leaves.

Chapter 43

I poked my head out at about 7:30 AM and saw the truck parked outside my tent. Excited, I jumped up to check it out. I figured I could use the truck for hauling scrap metal and recycling cans to make some cash. Having a truck is a must when trying to survive off scrapping and recycling.

I hopped in the truck, put the key in the ignition, pushed down on the brake and clutch, and rocked the stick shift into reverse. I gave the gas a slight push and pulled off on the brake at the same time as I was pushing in the clutch to try to put the truck in first gear. As I began to roll, I pulled up on the clutch a little too fast while giving it gas, and the truck stalled.

"Damn, I knew that was going to happen," I thought to myself, "that's why I don't like stick shifts."

As my nerves began to tremble and my legs began to shake, I tried to find that perfect rhythm of pull and push, as I attempted shifting again, hoping to avoid killing the engine a second time. I started moving and managed to make it into second and then third gear and back down to second as I pulled up to a stop sign. I was one block from where I'd started.

I pulled up along a big dumpster and began cleaning the truck out. I filled up a couple black trash bags full of leaves, garbage, empty oil canisters, and empty spray paint cans. There was a half-can of black spray paint that I saved to touch up the spots the last owner had missed.

I pulled back around the block and parked in the same spot where I'd started. I got out. It was probably about 8 AM at that point. Nobody was in sight. It was just an early Sunday morning. I thought to myself, "I'm going to do some touch up on the truck," but just as I started to shake the half-empty spray can, two Portland Police cars rolled up.

I pretended I didn't see them as I tried not to look spooked or suspicious. They both stopped and backed up. They got out and asked me what I was doing and if the vehicle was mine. I told them the story of how I'd just gotten it around 11 PM last night and how I'd only just then driven it around the block. I also told them that I hadn't yet had time to look into registering the truck in my name. I said that a buddy of mine had brought it to me in an emergency, really needing some cash so he could take his chick to turn herself in, and that I knew nothing else about the truck.

They told me that the truck had been reported stolen. I said, "This old truck? No way! It's obviously just been sitting somewhere for years. You could see that nobody would miss this truck."

They said that it was in fact stolen. At that point I was so fucking pissed. If it wasn't a setup, I don't know what it was. They began running my name and several warrants popped up from various other counties. I knew it was over. They'd trapped me. I was done. At that point, I assumed that I was not going to be getting let out for a good long while. They eventually indicted me on the Charger from a few days before, too.

Chapter 44

During the first hours after being arrested, I felt anger rising up in me because of how stupid I'd been to get myself in that situation. Then sadness took over at the thought of losing whatever belongings I had in my place. Eventually, I started to accept the thought of everyone ransacking and stealing all my stuff once again. Finally, the thought of not having any money, so no way to make bail, occurred to me.

That same thought progression happened every time I'd been arrested—what an emotional rollercoaster. But for some reason it's always much easier for me to sleep during the first couple weeks after an arrest. Maybe partly because I start coming down off all the drugs I've been on. That's also when I began to really think about everything that had led me to where I found myself.

I was stressing about my dog, Cleopatra. That was just before Sarah gave her to David. She was still back in the tent all by herself. I didn't have anyone to call to make sure she was safe. I knew that my belongings were goners because that's what happened every time I went to jail. It was always a free-for-all as soon as word got out that I'd been arrested. But mostly I was concerned about someone taking care of Cleopatra. I found out later that Sarah came and got her.

Next came a feeling of being powerless, trapped, and surrounded by a bunch of people I didn't want to be around, with nowhere to run. There's the fear that comes with trying to negotiate getting along with other inmates. On the outs, I could always separate myself from people or potential problems I didn't want to be

around, but in jail or prison, I had to learn a whole new way of dealing with people who crossed my path. It's usually best to just try to completely ignore everyone else and focus on yourself. I kept reminding myself that the whole thing was my fault, and that it would be over sooner or later.

As I sat on my bunk, I wondered to myself, "Do the people I've helped over the years even miss me? I wonder if they really care at all and if so, why hasn't anybody tried to contact me, sent me a letter, or come by for a visit? Are my son and his mom thinking about me? Are they waiting for me to come home?"

In general, I've come to the conclusion that people only care about you when you're giving them something they want, and then when that's done, you're just dust in the wind. I realized I really didn't have friends like I thought I did.

But I did care. I tried to show people a different way of doing things, like respecting others even when their ways were different from my own and trying to think that everyone deserves a chance. I'd learned that the only way to get through to people was by showing them directly and leading by example.

Most folks who I counseled and helped eventually caught on when I showed them that I didn't cheat and cut corners. I always tried to stay honest, respectful, patient, resourceful, open-minded, nonjudgmental, and willing to hear other's opinions, even though I may not have always agreed with what I was seeing or hearing.

After a couple of weeks, I found a lot of my answers coming from the Bible, reminding me of what happens when we stray from God. I realized God was the one holding the keys to my freedom and not only that, but when my trial came, he was not only the judge, but the DA, the attorney, and let's not forget the thirteen jury members listening to the case. But I knew I'd fucked up and was not going to win that battle even with God playing every role.

Chapter 45

I took the first deal the judge threw at me. I ended up sitting there in Inverness County jail for seven months before making my way to prison. I eventually moved into the treatment dorm for my last several months. I learned a lot about substance abuse—the psychological effects drugs have on the human brain and the damage they do to our bodies. It was the first time I ever received treatment for my drug addictions.

I knew it was working for me. I started to take advantage of my recovery and the time I was doing by getting my Parenting Certificate, Anger Management Certificate, and Treatment Readiness Certificate, and began preparing my mind for a sober lifestyle when I got out.

I'm near the end of my story and I was hoping for a beautiful ending. But just like most good books and movies, there's always something unexpected that happens when your main character thinks he or she has overcome their biggest fear or most challenging obstacle in life.

About eight months ago, I received a letter in the mail from Child Protective Services informing me that my son's mom had been through a domestic dispute in which she was struck by her boyfriend and that my son witnessed it all. They charged the man with child abuse. My son's mom later told me that her now-ex-boyfriend had beat her up and that he was in jail. She said she didn't want anything to do with the dude anymore, that he was a weirdo, and something along the lines of a sexual predator. One day she came home to find all her thongs, other underwear, and sex toys laid out in a row on the couch in the living room. The dude got off on doing that type of thing. It freaked her out.

I was so mad I wanted to take the dude out, but I didn't know who or where he was. I didn't even know what he looked like, so I didn't know what to look for, if by chance he ended up in the same prison as me.

For fourteen months I thought about how I'd handle the situation of running into him, if it were ever to occur. Then, with four months or less before my release, I woke up about 3 AM one morning to go to work in the kitchen. I checked the Call-Outs—the list of daily visits, video calls, classes, and programs. You could see what everyone on the unit was going to be up to that day. Suddenly, a name popped out at me. I thought to myself, "Why does that name look familiar?"

Then it occurred to me, that was the dude my son's mom was telling me about. I ran over and pulled out my paperwork from CPS and sure enough it was the same name. I walked over to his cell bunk number to see who he was and came to find out the dude had been in my unit for the last six months, maybe more. I'd never talked to him before, but I'd heard him talk to other people in the unit.

He never said anything at all to me, and suddenly I realized it was because he obviously had been ducking me, praying and hoping that I'd never find out who he was.

I talked to a few of my friends about who the dude was and they told me he was a real piece of shit, a weirdo, a crazy loudmouth who was always yelling out sexual comments to other dudes. They said his old cell mate had filed a grievance case against him for making gay and sexual comments. The guy had been run out of three other units at the prison. Nobody liked the guy.

I waited for the right time and then approached him. I asked if his name was Richard, and he said, "Yeah, I don't know why you're asking me, you already know who I am."

"Look, dude, I've never talked to you before. I don't know who the fuck you are."

I handed him the letter that Child Protective Services had sent me. He looked it over then said, "Yeah, so what?"

"So what? So what? What happened? Don't you have anything to say to me about what happened?"

"All you need to know is that nothing happened physically to your son, it was just that he saw me put hands on Brandy. She and I are still together though, and she's been telling me on the phone about the letters you've sent her saying how much you want to be back in their lives, how you've been telling her that you've changed for the better, and that you're ready to make up for the lost time not being there for your son. But I've got to tell you, it's not going to happen, OK?"

That was a shock. I just took the letter back from the dude and walked away. I wrote Brandy to let her know that I was not writing to her anymore. I'd never received anything positive back from her anyway. I'd sent Christmas cards, birthday cards, letters, and messages on the tablet and I never got a positive reply from her or any reassurance that things would be better when I got out. She'd only say enough to keep stringing me along.

Even though I wasn't getting the responses I wanted, Brandy had me thinking things were getting better anyway. Not once did she say she was still with that dude or that he was in the same prison, much less in the same unit with me, and only fifteen bunks away from mine for the last six months or more.

I was all fucked up in the head thinking to myself about that weirdo dude knowing who I was and that he had been watching me all that time while Brandy was telling him about all my letters.

What was I going to do? I decided to take the legal route and contact my son's caseworker and attempt to get legal custody so that the Richard guy wouldn't get out and think he was going to play daddy with my son. I didn't trust the guy and saw him as a threat to my child. I was going to do whatever it took to protect my son.

That became my main focus. Brandy and Richard just might be perfect for each other, but my son didn't need to be around that kind of negative lifestyle. It felt like everything I'd been working on had crumbled to the ground. Mentally, I was just trying to do the mature thing and look at the situation as another life lesson. I was trying to understand that God had bigger plans, and something better could come out of the situation. I just had to take the right steps when dealing with the problem, so I didn't put myself in a worse situation.

Chapter 46

I don't feel like my story is anything worth bragging about. I'm just trying to explain this spiritual journey I've been on throughout my life, which has actually been a real trip. I've had some fun, but I'm not happy with how things turned out. There have been a lot of weird, negative experiences. I feel like I haven't had complete control over my life, no matter how hard I've tried. But ultimately, I take responsibility for my actions anyway.

I've learned from the negativity, the uneven quality of my life, and now the loss of my freedom. I feel like I've come out on the other side a stronger man and have learned some valuable skills about life that I can now teach to my son.

I also want to apologize to anyone I may have badly impacted, anyone whose property I may have destroyed, and anyone else I may have upset emotionally with my poor decision making. I'm going to do everything in my power to stay clean from now on and be a force for good.

When I get out, I want to first focus on whatever I need to do to establish a relationship with my son. My steps will include finding housing, getting treatment, and keeping up with the requirements of my probation. If I can find a good job, things should continue to get even better. Eventually, I might want to move away with my son and his mom to Alaska or some other remote place to live off the land and be free from all the temptations and destruction we're surrounded in the city.

Chapter 47

I think music can really define who a person is. When I was in Hawaii, Brandy and I were sending our favorite songs back and forth, trying to communicate our love for each other, especially being so far apart. Emotionally we were using music to express our love and to connect with and learn about each other. Music and lyrics can be a magical way to communicate.

Even now that I'm in prison, I still send Brandy songs to let her know how I feel about her and to engage in topics that I can't find the right words for. Again, trying to make a long-distance relationship work can be more challenging than almost anything. One day I'll have a place of my own with a super system so I can turn up my music as loud as I want, the same with my car.

If I had to pick one thing to have with me every day, besides my son, it would be music. If the world would end all of a sudden, I think music would be the biggest loss. I wonder if there's a way we could save every song ever created on a giant USB stick on a satellite or something. It would be amazing if we were able to send all that music through the universe, for anybody out there to hear—that is, if we don't already.

One night on my bunk I fell asleep with my music playing through my headphones. It was a new experience for me. All I could hear in my sleep state were the beats, no words. Songs would come on and I'd recognize them, but somehow it sounded way better than when I was awake. It was kind of like being underwater, listening to my music. What that means to me is that even though your body is asleep, your consciousness and your soul are awake and experiencing everything that is going on around you.

Chapter 48

Every day I caught myself staring at the ceiling, thinking to myself, "Is this the way it's supposed to be? Is it me and my family? Or is it just me? Am I here on this planet just so Brandy can have a son? Do I love her for birthing my son? Or can I love her unconditionally? Should I do everything in my power to make the relationship work even though I get the feeling she doesn't want me around? I don't feel any love coming from her at all. Is that my fault for being gone for so long? My gut is telling me to just leave her alone, that things will never work out for me and her. There are a lot of things about her I'll never understand, but I want to be there for my son! No matter what!"

I was so confused and really stressed out wondering what things were going to be like when I got out. I didn't know what else to do besides count the days. Every song that came on reminded me of Brandy and my son. I kept waiting for Brandy to tell me she wanted me to come home, that she loved me and missed me. I hoped that one day Brandy would bring my son to visit me, but I also knew that most likely wasn't going to happen.

I'd set up video visits, but Brandy would say she couldn't figure out how to accept my requests. I knew I'd fucked up, and I knew Brandy was still mad at me and she was probably treating me that way to show me how much pain I'd caused her and my son.

I was sorry that I wasn't ready to be a father, that I'd run from my fears, and that I was not prepared for having a kid. But considering everything I'd been through with Brandy, I just wanted her to put our differences aside so we could give our son everything he needed and deserved, which was a loving, responsible father, and a loving, kind mother. I wished that I could have been there for Brandy the way that she needed me to be. But I was ready to acknowledge her pain, and ready to accept her love, and give her all my love. It had been so long since things had been going in the wrong direction for us, and I wondered if it was all just too late.

Chapter 49

I'd been incarcerated for just about two years. In those two years I'd stayed clean and sober. Considering how available drugs are in prison, that meant something. My mind was made up—I was done with drugs! I was ready to take on life's responsibilities, and most importantly, as part of that, to be the best father I could be for my son. I wanted to set a good example for the people around me and become a respected man in society.

Since I'd been down, I'd tried everything in my power to rebuild my relationship with Brandy. It took a lot of patience and empathy to hear her out. But I'd been open-minded and all ears to everything she wanted to express to me. She was slowly coming around to the idea that I should have a role in our son's life and it felt like she was going to give me another chance. It was unknown at the time what the relationship between us would be, but as I expressed to her in a letter, I was hoping that we could somehow work things out.

I sent the first part of this book to Brandy, everything up to the last couple chapters. I believe it helped her understand a little more about me and all the hardships I'd been through.

I sent her another letter and asked her to try to be open-minded, because I had to get some things off my chest. It wasn't that I was mad or anything, I just needed some reassurance that everything was going to be OK when I got out. I wanted her to know that I was planning a new way of living. It's really hard to rebuild a family from behind bars. There was no other way to show her that I meant what I was saying. That I wasn't just talking out of my ass like most men do when they're in prison. She always said that we (men in prison) all say the same things. I wanted to show her that wasn't true when I got out.

Brandy told me on a call that at the same time I was writing my letter to her, she was writing a long one to me too, so that I could know more about her life growing up, and how she felt about everything. I was really looking forward to receiving the letter. I was feeling really hopeful that everything would continue to get better for our little family.

Postscript

I was released from prison on July 3, 2024. I'm writing this on July 12, 2025. I've been out just over a year, and I'd say it's been a very productive time so far. I stuck to my plans of constructing a normal, healthy, positive life. I've had to literally put blinders on and lower my shoulders and move with force to accomplish my goals and responsibilities. I have tried to avoid all distractions from the path of success that I'm on.

Right after I got out my mom contacted me after thirty years. She friended me on Facebook. I accepted and we ended up writing to each other, but it was really awkward. I spent all that time, ever since leaving Southern California as a kid, just trying to forget about her and that whole situation.

She wrote to me with an attitude like I was supposed to be excited to hear from her and that I'd want to rebuild a relationship with her after all that time. I realized I was kind of trying to do something like that with my own son, so I tried to be accepting, but I couldn't find the will to try to rebuild our relationship. It was like trying to welcome a stranger into my life but I didn't want to let anyone into my life who might negatively impact my positive state of mind.

I put her on the back burner. Mostly I just don't engage. She's still in Moreno Valley. I asked if she knew where my dad was but she said she hadn't heard from him in ages. It would be nice to know where he's living and to be able to someday ask him some questions about what happened in the past. My parents were one of the main

reasons I'd gotten into drugs, so I could bury the feelings I had about them.

My mom wasn't in contact with my brother and sister, but I know, through limited contact with people from back in the day, that my brother became a pot grower in the Humboldt mountains, and my sister lives in Fortuna, California. When we were kids my sister was always singing in her room. She'd have mini talent shows with her friends, doing karaoke. She always wanted to be a professional singer and performer. Later in her life she actually made it onto the TV show *American Idol,* but I guess she didn't win or anything.

Things didn't go as planned with Brandy. I tried everything I could to be a part of my son's life. They did move to Portland to be closer to me and because Brandy had some medical stuff to take care of up here. They actually moved into an apartment building near where I live now. I got to spend Christmas with them last December, which was something I'd been wanting to experience for a long time. I went shopping and bought some gifts for my son—a bunch of video games and computer stuff and some cool lights for his room. He said he liked everything I gave him.

After all that time, my son really seemed like he accepted me. But Brandy said I was love-bombing him. She didn't like that I was trying my best to fix things and make everything normal. She flipped out and got mad about me for talking to chicks on Facebook. We weren't even together or anything. I just started a new account and looked up some of the women I knew from high school. Brandy made a big deal out of it, saying I was more interested in other people than my son, even though I'd spend all of my extra time with him.

Brandy told me to just leave them alone, so I stayed away for a few weeks. Eventually I went to go play basketball with my son. We were shooting hoops when I explained to him that I loved him and wanted to be a part of his life but that I was having disagreements with his mom and that was why I hadn't been around recently.

Later he told Brandy that I'd blamed her for everything, which wasn't what I'd said. She flipped out and told me she'd call me when I could see him again, but it's been two months now and I haven't heard anything from her.

I decided I can't fight her anymore, so I've just concentrated on my programs and work. I know if I try to see my son it will just make things worse and I'll never be able to see him. I just hope he'll let me know when he's ready to see me again. Brandy has full legal custody, and she never asked for child support, so she says I don't have any right to be in his life. I wouldn't be surprised if she got back with that guy from my unit and moved down to Salem.

That first day out of prison was crazy. There was so much to do—checking in with probation and going to Bridge to Change for transitional housing. I also went shopping for clothes at Goodwill and got shoes and a couple pairs of pants and shirts. My mentor and I went to Southeast Works where I met with my caseworker, and she helped me out with a smartphone and a couple months' phone service.

We talked about future employment. I told her I wanted to become a mentor. She suggested I wait until after I moved out of the Bridge to Change house so I could spend some time really thinking about whether that was something I wanted to do. I agreed, but I'd already made up my mind that helping others was what I wanted to do in the future. I think that's what God was trying to tell me all along, it was just the drugs and all that were making it hard for me to hear.

After a week out and getting used to being back in society and dealing with public transportation and people everywhere, I began my pursuit of happiness. I went down to a day labor temp agency and signed up. I was working the very next day for a construction company doing clean up. They liked me and the way I worked and asked me to come back. I ended up working for that company for three weeks, but I wanted a full-time job and didn't want to be breaking my back for a company I didn't really care about.

I got on an online job database and started applying for jobs all over the place. I have kitchen skills that I learned in prison, so I started applying for cook positions and right away I got a job at International House of Pancakes, the one located at Cascade Parkway near the Portland airport.

I worked there for about ten months before I started really thinking about my future and what I wanted to do with the rest of my life for employment. I definitely was not wanting to make IHOP my career and the longer I stayed there, the more it began to suck me in and consume me.

I love making food but being a cook at a restaurant and dealing with customer service requires mental strength and patience. You're working in a place where everyone hates their job and has a bad attitude because they don't want to be there. The negativity of the people I was working with really rubbed me the wrong way. It was making me very uncomfortable, like I was walking on eggshells.

In February they cut my hours to just two days a week—Saturday and Sunday—the two busiest days of the week, and the most stressful. I worked about six hours a day, so only twelve hours a week, and that lasted about three months.

It wasn't enough for me to survive on, with restitution payments, cell phone bills, food, and needing to buy a bus pass to get to work and back. So, I started to take advantage of all that time off and got connected with Central City Concern, a low-income housing organization. I eventually got a job working with them, and they helped me become a Certified Recovery Mentor and Peer Support Wellness Specialist.

After completing the training, I got registered with the Mental Health and Addiction Certification Board of Oregon. Now I can work anywhere in the state as a CRM/PWS. It felt so good to begin a career in a field that I actually have hard, real, lived experience in. I can take what's happened to me and share it with others who are struggling to find a way out of addiction, pain, and misery. I can now look at my life as training that God put me through, not only to make me stronger but so I'd be able to help other people.

After leaving the Bridge to Change house, I moved into the Estates Apartment Building downtown, joining the Housing Regulatory Relief program. I graduated from that program in eight months—another achievement that felt really good. As part of my court-mandated Strategic Treatment and Engagement Program I also had to complete a fourteen-month long treatment-based program called Moral Reconation Therapy. I know that maybe sounds like bullshit, but it actually all helped me a lot.

While I was living in the Estates, I met someone very special to me. Her name is Samantha, and she's fulfilled all the wishes I've ever had about finding a woman who loves and cares for me. She's also just gotten out of prison.

Samantha and I got a studio apartment together. It's on the outskirts of town, but we're the first people to ever live in it, so everything is really new and clean. We like to take the MAX train downtown to the river. Sometimes we just sit there all day together, right next to the Steel Bridge. From that spot, I can see where I used to live as a homeless person in a tent for a time, but that seems like another world to me now.

Acknowledgements

The author would like to thank Harrell Fletcher, Laura Glazer, Virgil Shaw, and everyone who played an important role in helping publish this book.

Some People Press would like to thank the following people for their support of the project: Lakshmi and Hari Cianculli, Jay Platt, Marcy Freedman, Josh Donen, Chris Johanson, Miranda July, Beatrice Red Star Fletcher, Sarah Minnick, James Hanley, Lindy Laurence (from Rational Unicorn), Karleigh Frisbie Brogan, Kristi Garced, Gretchen Dykstra, Sarah Mooney, the staff at Columbia River Correctional Institution, and the participants in the writing workshop.

About the Author

William Shawn Tillman was born in Southern California and raised up north in Humboldt County. While incarcerated, he wrote his autobiography in an attempt to share his journey and spiritual awakening. Tillman has overcome some tough moments and hopes that by telling his story he can help others who are struggling with what life might be throwing at them, including homelessness, addiction, feeling lost, and losing faith. Regardless of anyone's religious beliefs, Tillman wants everyone to know that there is a higher power, and it resides within each of us.

About Some People Press

Some People Press publishes autobiographies by formerly incarcerated writers, as well as books on art and other subjects. We challenge the idea that only certain people—with the right education, experiences, and connections—can be published authors. Instead, we encourage writers to use their existing skills and to "write what you know." Writers develop their work at their own pace, with the support and feedback of their peers and at weekly meetings with project leaders and visitors. Some People Press is supported by book sales and contributions via Venmo @somepeoplepress.

Same Time Series

Enjoy the Ride! is the fifth book in the Same Time series. Many of the writers in this series took part in the autobiographical writing and publishing project at Columbia River Correctional Institution, a minimum-security prison in Northeast Portland, Oregon. During weekly classes they workshopped their writing with fellow participants and with visiting writers, publishers, and artists, including Miranda July, Chris Johanson, Constance Debré, Jim Drain, and Laura Moulton. All profits from sales of books in the Same Time series are split evenly between Some People Press and the author.

Titles in the Same Time Series

Smile Now, Cry Later by Terry James

How Long Is Five Minutes? by Arron Magar

Worth It! by Joey Lucero

The Blacksmith by Juliano Miller

Enjoy the Ride! by William Shawn Tillman